German Soccer Passing Drills

Hyballa | te Poel

GERMAN SOCCER PASSING DRILLS

More than 100 Drills from the Pros

Meyer & Meyer Sport

Original title: Modernes Passspiel
Translation: AAA Translations, St. Louis, Missouri

German Soccer Passing Drills

Maidenhead: Meyer & Meyer Sport (UK) Ltd., 2015
ISBN 978-1-78255-048-8

© 2015 by Meyer & Meyer Sport (UK) Ltd.
Aachen, Auckland, Beirut, Cairo, Cape Town, Dubai, Hägendorf, Hong Kong, Indianapolis, Manila,
New Delhi, Singapore, Sydney, Teheran, Vienna

 Member of the World Sport Publishers' Association (WSPA)

Total production by: Print Consult GmbH, Germany, Munich
ISBN 978-1-78255-048-8
E-Mail: info@m-m-sports.com
www.m-m-sports.com

ACKNOWLEDGMENTS

To my sons Nils and Jens and my wife Isabel, who for several years have gifted me the "free" time to create this book, and to my DFB soccer instructors, trainers, and lecturers Gero Bisanz † (former DFB chief training instructor, lecturer at the German Sports College Cologne, and trainer at the 1. FC Cologne soccer club) and Dr. Gunnar Gerisch (former director of the soccer department at the German Sports College Cologne and lecturer at the Hennes-Weisweiler Academy), who have taught me "the game" at the highest level. But my sincere thanks also goes to my friend and co-author Peter, who knows what it means to work together on this book reliably and constantly for several years.

Our great and everlasting respect goes to Eduard Feldbusch, who made himself available day and night for meetings and who rendered our hundreds of hand-drawn sketches into professional graphics with such an unbelievable amount of "soccer feeling."

Hans-Dieter te Poel

www.tepoel.eu

I dedicate this book to my father Hans-Joachim, who now watches the game of games from the heavenly stands.

Peter Hyballa

www.peterhyballa.org

TABLE OF CONTENTS

FOREWORD

All ball circulation is based on a good passing game. Many recent examples show that this can result in successful top-level soccer. Within the scope of their playing philosophy, even the national team constantly works on the passing game and combines this with group and team-tactical measures. To implement variable and efficient team play at the highest level, teams must be able to quickly open up space. In particular, this can be done with precise, well-timed, flat, hard, and vertical passes.

A successful passing game relies on foundations laid by targeted, variable, and intensive training. Training units on the field are extremely important for coaches and players as their teams evolve and try to reach the highest level. In *German Soccer Passing Drills*, Peter Hyballa and Hans-Dieter te Poel lay the foundation to develop a successful passing game.

In this book, the authors examine many types of passes and performance factors that can lay the foundation through training. As such the book *German Soccer Passing Drills* is a training model and is a true mine of information for any coach.

In 2015, the authors Peter Hyballa and Hans-Dieter te Poel published a second German book on the passing game. This work includes contributions from experts of the most diverse areas of performance-oriented soccer and applied sports science. The different perspectives of the what and how in the international passing game are presented using focused interviews; there is also a large number of additional drills and different types of plays.

Together these two books represent a handbook for all coaches and trainers with an interest in relevant, detailed, and intensive goal-oriented training and the advancement of their players.

Hans-Dieter Flick

Sporting director of the German Soccer Federation (DFB) and former assistant coach of the German national soccer team, World Champion 2014 in Brazil

01

PRELIMINARY REMARKS

01 PRELIMINARY REMARKS

Currently, there is much discussion about the passing game, particularly in professional soccer. Whether it is a tool that makes team play possible or enables the team to keep possession or is intended to create dominance on the field, all of these demands on the passing game are intended to result in winning the game. It can be that simple!

But how and with which drills and variations does a coach or instructor, together with young and adult players, develop an attractive and expedient passing game? Is it specifically as a part of soccer training that focuses on the development, improvement, and optimization of performance, or is it all just a matter of talent, even magic, or solely the realization of a plan?

Based on individual training practice, ambitious coaches and instructors are always on the lookout for new suggestions as well as validation of one's own passing philosophy. The authors therefore offer their colleagues a kind of training model for a modern passing game that can provide new ideas for their own training on the field. So does this mean more of the same old self-knitted rudiments and recipes for a modern passing game? Not at all!

The book is divided into six chapters, including the foreword by the German national team assistant coach, Hans-Dieter Flick.

In chapter 2 the coach and instructor learns about the essential game-theoretical considerations that the training model, the Hyballa/te Poel Passing Puzzle IQ® (see chapter 4) is based on.

Chapter 3 focuses on the question of whether a pass, is a pass, is a pass, as is often the mindset in training and instruction and de facto in soccer. This issue is analyzed and outlined based on

- the content of chapter 2,
- the requirement profiles and specific complexity of soccer,
- the necessary emotional control during the passing game, and
- the players' critical thinking ability.

In chapter 4, we outline our complex Hyballa/te Poel Passing Puzzle IQ® intended to contribute to the coach's and instructor's ever-present quest for the "highest passing quality." But it also includes additional performance-determining factors and always takes into account the *coach's and instructor's* attention to time spent selecting drills and types of play and collective self-referential communication (of team or rather group). For the players, competition and training play an important role in the desired positive development of fast, precise, variable, and creative passing within the group: There are many small soccer worlds!

In subchapter 4, the reader learns why we chose the form of a puzzle and why—see subchapter 4.2—this can be easily applied to practical training using passing grids (framework). In this regard, a lot of emphasis is placed on dovetailing practical training with the game's situational context. Subchapter 4.2.1 shows how to coach this on the field with the innovative 3-action system.

In subchapter 4.3, the reader is presented with 20 types of passes (puzzles) that can be directly implemented on the practice field: organization, process, coaching, and variations. These should be integrated without restriction and combined with other performance-determining factors (e. g., *passing fitness*). The desired playing creativity that coaches, instructors, and players are meant to achieve in working with the Passing Puzzle® is referred to as "IQ" (*passing intelligence*).

The different parts of the picture, 20 puzzles on the surface and 6 puzzles in the deep, represent the demands of competitive play.

The puzzles are presented to the reader in the form of shelves with materials such as in a hardware store. In a well-organized hardware store, these are fully stocked so that someone, whether an amateur or a professional, can pick and choose at their own whim. This image helps the reader to comprehend the material in this book.

In this regard the subchapters 4.3.18 (*Tiqui-Taca* Special—Rondos) and 4.3.20 (Special Goalie Passing With Goalie Trainer Marco Knoop) provide two particularly excellent puzzles with scope and attention to detail that have never been seen before. To this effect the *Rondos* for perfect compact foot and passing technique and goalie passing for professional goalie training are based on current empirical findings on goalkeeping.

In subchapter 4.4 we use our passing and playing philosophy to show how to teach implementation of the same on the field to one's own team, in this case a professional team, using the example of the narrow 1-4-3-3.

Subchapter 4.5 describes, discusses, analyzes, and interprets current insights on the question of how to implement the puzzle pieces in training and condenses many teaching and coaching methods and rules in the passing game into a comprehensive chart categorized by motor, cognitive, and mixed (linked) components. We refer to the individual Passing Puzzles® and the connections with the selected performance factors, technique, tactics (including *passing intelligence*) and fitness (*endurance*). By using these methodical components the coach or instructor is able to make his passing training goal-oriented, precise, and always diverse.

Chapter 5 offers a simple summary of essential suppositions and complements as well as quotes from colleagues who, in our opinion, have made forward-looking statements on these topics.

The book ends with extensive literary references and picture credits. The interested reader can browse here and find additional information for his training instruction. To that effect these parts of the book are not only significant as proof and a brainstorming hub for assertions and featured graphic work, charts, and pictures, but they are also intended to firmly and emphatically reinforce and express the necessity of bibliography, even in technical soccer books and articles about soccer.

The following key applies to all of the independently created graphics and images, and an additional key is located in chapter 4.3.20 for *goalie passing*.

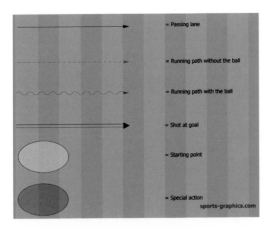

Fig. 1: Key for the following graphics and images

The literary language, particularly in chapter 4, has been chosen in order to work with metaphors, images, code words and descriptions, explanations, analyses, and assessments within training and instruction on the field and in the gym. It is intended to support coaching in soccer language, much like getting advice at the hardware store. Like the hardware store customer, the reader makes his own choices! Enjoy!

Hans-Dieter te Poel and Peter Hyballa

Cologne/Leverkusen, May 2014

02

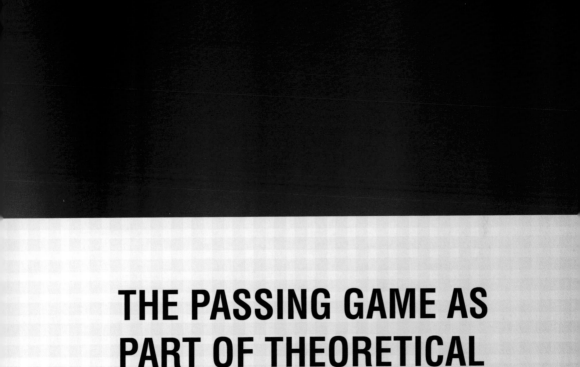

THE PASSING GAME AS PART OF THEORETICAL GAME CONSIDERATIONS

THE PASSING GAME AS PART OF THEORETICAL GAME CONSIDERATIONS

"I often ask myself: What is this or that team trying to achieve? Do you only want to shoot goals from standard situations? To me soccer is passing, dribbling, combinations, in other words, playing. (...) There are teams who are happy when they win. Here at Barça we have a different passion. We want to play soccer that gets people excited. We will stick to this philosophy, no matter what. (...) In other clubs all the focus is on winning, even in the youth leagues. In our youth teams we focus on learning. There are kids using their heads, passing and playing. Our model is the one Johann Cruyff brought to this club. It's all about playing soccer, every damn day!"

(Xavi, FC Barcelona, quote from Schulze-Marmeling 2013, pg. 165-166)

In his article "The Thinker" (2013, pg. 68-69), the sports editor Jörg Wolfrum quotes the former FC Barcelona soccer instructor Gerardo Martino (master coach in Argentina and Paraguay) on the playing style of his former club under Pep Guardiola. Wolfrum uses these appreciatory words: "Technique, possession, superior numbers" and: "Passing is a requirement for good soccer" (2013, pg. 69).

Considering FC Barcelona's average possession of 63% and 600-700 passes per game during the 2008/2009 season, this seems to be a plausible assumption at first glance (see UEFA 2012a, pg. 14). The UEFA's statistics for the Champions League even show an average possession of 73.3% and 800 passes per game during the 2010/2012 season. These statistics show that FC Barcelona has managed to continuously increase their possession over their opponents during the four years under head coach Pep Guardiola.

Pep Guardiola has taken the philosophy of long possession to FC Bayern Munich. Whether or not this soccer philosophy helped him to secure the early Bundesliga championship in March 2014 is still under debate. The April 7, 2014 edition of the sports magazine *kicker* published statistical information clearly showing that compared to the previous 2012/2013 season, the FC Bayern Munich pro soccer team under its new head coach had undergone the following changes in the Champions League games:

- From 54.4% possession during the 2012/2013 CL to 69.8% during the 2013/2014 CL.
- From 515 passes per game during the 2012/2013 CL to 725 passes during the 2013/2014 CL.
- From 359 touches in the opposing half during the 2012/2013 CL to 550 touches in the opposing half during the 2013/2014 CL.
- One third of the goals conceded by FC Bayern Munich during the 2013/2014 season were scored by their opponents on counterattacks. Under the soccer instructor Jupp Heynckes, the team listed this many conceded goals from counters within two regulation playing periods, and no other Bundesliga team can currently top that high number of conceded goals from counters.
- Nearly every third corner awarded to FC Bayern Munich is taken with a short *flat pass*.
- On average, FC Bayern Munich's last defensive line is located near the centerline during possession. That is about 16 to 23 feet closer to the opposing goal than under soccer instructor Jupp Heynckes. This creates more space for fast attacks (especially with *up-and-over passes* and *into-space*) for the opposing team.

Add to that the parameter for the degree of pass accuracy of FC Bayern Munich in games during the 2013/2014 season in all competitions (Bundesliga championships, DFB Cup, and CL), and you get a pass completion rate of 88.7% in the Bundesliga and 90.3% in the CL. By comparison: Borussia Dortmund has a pass completion rate of 78.6% during the ongoing 2013/2014 Bundesliga season (pg. 45).

However, a causal relationship between a constructive possession philosophy using the passing game methods and guaranteed success *cannot* be established (see UEFA 2012a, pg. 14). A current study by Cologne sport scientist Dr. J. Mesters and Bayer 04 Leverkusen's longtime fitness trainer and performance diagnostician Dr. Holger Broich emphasizes this empirical fact. But both sport scientists from the Cologne Sports College (*momentum*) also point out that in teams like FC Barcelona or Bayern Munich that have a touch percentage of approximately 70%, the playing quality of the team increases considerably, and the likelihood of scoring lots of points goes up tangentially (see von Nocks 2014, pg. 16-17).

These findings then beg the question whether high pass completion and possession rates should not, in general, be more likely to form the basis for attacking play rather than being the objective (see FIFA 2011, pg. 63; Eichler 2014, pg. 23). Japan, for instance, had 620 successful passes in a game against New Zealand during the FIFA U17 world championships in Mexico—92% of all the team's passes (see FIFA 2011, pg. 39), and the midfielder Thiago (FC Bayern Munich) set a new world record on February 1, 2014 in a Bundesliga game against Eintracht Frankfurt with 185 passes (172 of these to a teammate).

However, based on the available statistical data, the great importance of passing play to the quality of a soccer game at present is a given. [1]

But what does that say about the "essence" of the passing game? Looking at its emergence from a historical game perspective gains insights that can be of particular significance, especially for imparting the essence of passing in training and competition.

Arroyo (1992, 2002) points out that with the introduction of a modified offside rule, what used to be a wild and chaotic battle for the ball with considerable physical damage is changing into a game with increasing cognitive aspects. These are reflected

---

[1] To the interested reader we particularly recommend the sources UEFA (2012a and b), FIFA (2010 and 2011), and, for German readers, the süddeutsche.de (about passing game in the Bundesliga 2012/2013 season). These are marked accordingly in the literary references. Regarding the problems with position detection systems, passing statistics from comparisons between countries, and video analysis, we refer the German reader to Siegle, Geisel & Lames (2012, 278-282), Memmert (2013 a and b), and Lames (2012).

in the intelligent learning processes the players use to regard each other and read the ideas of their teammates and opponents. The first offside rule stated that a player is offside only when he is in front of the horizontal line that the ball formed to the touchline (see Raads 2009, pg. 17). The result was that forward or backward passing was not advantageous, and the vigor and willpower of individual players became game-determining parameters. The modified offside rule, on the other hand, incidentally changed the way players moved in space and time in relation to themselves and their teammates. The new technical element, the pass, thereby became the most important design mechanism for anticipating, planning, and implementing. The battle-like game turned into today's *interactive game* with its inexhaustible creativity that finds its equivalent in soccer training and competition, especially nowadays, in the communicative character of passing play:

> *"During a game all players must speak the same soccer language (...). That means that the pass cannot be viewed as just a technical-tactical skill, but also as social interaction and nonverbal communication with a teammate."*
> (Wein 2004, pg. 7)[2]

The following example from recent Bundesliga history supports this assertion. At age 34 and after a nearly six-month hiatus from competing, the former Leverkusen fullback and nine-time national team player Manuel

Friedrich briefly came in as a sub in a game against the reigning German Champion and Champions League winner FC Bayern Munich. On November 25, 2013, the *Frankfurter Allgemeine Zeitung* analyzed his playing effort as follows:

"The lack of playing practice was apparent whenever Friedrich had his foot on the ball, when he was supposed to contribute to the game build-up. In those moments he

---

2   Here the authors forgo a description of passing, shooting, crossing, heading, throwing in, and ball control techniques and instead refer the reader to the detailed practice-oriented executions by Bisanz/Gerisch (2013, pg. 332-363), Titz/ Dooley (2010, pg. 10-12), Buschmann/Kollath &Tritschoks (2005, Volume 1), Kollath (2000), and many national and international empiric studies on the impact of biomechanical parameters (such as center of mass (CoM), impulse of the thigh, foot speed, run up speed, soccer shoes) on the passing or rather shot velocity and precision of youth players and men at the highest playing levels (see Barfield 1998; Juárez et al. 2011; Naito et al. 2010).

seemed quite overwhelmed. 'I didn't have the same ideas as my teammates. At times it looked pretty ghastly. But I fought my way into the game and it got better with every tackle. My timing is back and defensively I did alright.'"

In this context, the implementation of the offside rule is more evidence of how rule changes with a specific intent, in this case limiting delays by the goalie, in recent years resulted in the development of the playing (and passing) goalie (libero).

Raads (2009, pg. 18) summarizes the phenomenal importance of the passing game for our soccer game in a very succinct and vivid quote:

"The game's socio-affective character could not be emphasized more plainly. Soccer is about nothing less than collective communication and collective fit. When the chemistry between players is such that the ball makes it into the opposing goal, it is a special achievement of collective nonverbal communication skills. Such special achievements also produce special emotions, namely the exact ecstatic occurrences that can be seen in stadiums among players and fans. When there are frequent misunderstandings between players and subsequently goals by the opposing team and losses, the disappointment is as great as the joy in playing. A game can be won with a single opportune action and can also be lost due to a single misunderstanding. Thus soccer is a reflection of the phylogenetic deeply anchored drive for collective communication ability, and thereby a reflection of the desire for functioning relationships (Bischof 1985). One pre-eminent condition for soccer to be successful is the way people interact with each other and how they FIT together. Fighting together has little chance for success if people aren't compatible and don't connect well."[3]

Lucien Favre, former Swiss national team player and head coach of the premiere league Borussia Mönchengladbach also emphasizes the major importance of having a rapport with others to develop his team's tactical variability:

---

3   This example illustrates that this approach to soccer training has many connections to modern sports educational schemes in Germany. The educational perspective "cooperate, compete, communicate" that is a primary component of play-based learning in educational schemes at schools and universities is established by responding to the needs of teammates during soccer training. Thus soccer training in schools could help require and facilitate the collective communication processes in, for instance, youth competitive soccer, choosing to cooperate and perform via concrete teamwork in a specific situation (see Hänsel/Baumgärtner 2014, pg. 37-62).

"But it usually takes lots of time and you must be willing to get to know your players better."

(Quoted by Uwe Marx and Richard Leipold in the *Frankfurter Allgemeine Zeitung*, Nov. 22, 2013, pg. 29)

According to this, the team sport of soccer is primarily about information brokering and processing and personality system interactions, with fundamental motives and different approaches to team or group leadership that the coach or instructor must consider (see Kuhl 2001; Rybicki 2013). It must also be pointed out at this time that the aesthetic component of a soccer game under competitive conditions (and in different cultures) can play a considerable role in observing and analyzing. But because it is multidimensional, it defies rational conceptualities and currently has not been pursued further. Taken as a whole, the cited analysis of topics shows the coaches, instructors, players and students that knowledge and behavior can correlate (see Abel 2004, pg. 85). To develop high-quality communication patterns in soccer training, it is generally important that the cognitive content—for example, our passing game—is successfully demonstrated in practice because it can then be learned and automated more quickly by the players (see Spitzer 2006). This can develop into stable patterns that can become a team's quasi-symbols; for instance, the *Fohlenelf* (the foals) as a synonym for the fast and successful counterattacking soccer of 1970s Germany, or *Tiqui-Taca* for the possession and opponent-dominating world soccer in recent years (see chapter 4.3.18).

A team's recognizable symbol can be derived from psychology and interpreted as a symbol with a definite identity because it is based on "successful comprehension and execution of passing performance" (Raads 2009, pg. 45).

"We steadied ourselves incredibly fast and worked extremely passionately to fix what happened. The success has helped us."

(Jos Luhukay, head coach Hertha BSC quoted in kicker, Sept. 9, 2013, 74, pg. 13)

In addition, it is extremely important for practice and instruction that the Passing Puzzle® (see chapter 4) is complete and geared to technical and tactical abilities and skills, such as offering support to teammates, getting open, and shielding the ball. It is also important that these abilities and skills are practiced and learned consistently as a group (see Roxburgh 2012, pg. 9). The following three examples taken from professional soccer elucidate the necessity of practicing as a group:

- *"The boys are not satisfied and are working day and night to develop a better mutual understanding and to improve their individual performance."*

  (Head Coach Benno Möhlmann, FSV Frankfurt, quoted by Helms in kicker, Aug. 8, 2013, pg. 9)

- *"I don't have any ready professionals, but rather boys that have to be worked every day because they still have too many unsettled resources"* ... *The open body position, the correct leg, eyes in playing direction – these are opportunities for winning precious seconds. We have to learn to play clean and precise under pressure."*

  (Head Coach Torsten Lieberknecht, Eintracht Braunschweig, quoted by Bernreuther in kicker, July 22, 2013, pg. 31)

- *"The one who plays for himself plays for the opposition."*

  (Helenio Herrera, deceased Argentine soccer coach and creator of the   Catenaccio; n.y. and w.o.)

However, the path to the passing game that reflects action speed, goal threat, and resource economics presupposes "efficient algorithms" based on "dynamic patterns"– dynamic because the game possesses an infinite breadth of "passing elements" that should be developed consciously and unconsciously in the very early stages of soccer training to make a career as a professional player possible (Raads 2009, pg. 49, 51). That is why the book's topics far exceed content-related (and mostly logical) communication between coach and player or player and coach and specifically includes communication problems and their resolution in terms of collective, effective, stable, and progressive action (and the preliminary interpretations of all who are part of a game that continues to evolve). And how do coach and player recognize that communication problems exist? When thinking outweighs feeling and players are more focused on processing their mistakes than a successful pass that facilitates a good subsequent action (e.g., a shot at goal). The following chapters therefore put a lot of emphasis on the situational game derivation of different types of passes that are characterized by pre-, main-, and post-actions (i.e., efficient contact) in the sense of theoretical executions. Thus classified, the pass is a function of collective, not individual, behavior within the team that is most often expressed in the flow of play. In this context, under consideration of the perspective of behavioral psychology, Raads (2009, pg. 45-46) emphasizes that in the passing game every player has three roles: the emotional, the dynamic, and the logical role. "[E]ach of these roles has structuring character for the semiotic process of collective behavior."[4]

> *"Each player also thinks for the other one and is prepared to take on varying roles, sometimes the water boy, sometimes the star."*
> (Pep Guardiola, Bayern Munich, quoted by Rybicki 2013, pg. KuS 1)

The underlying idea presumes that purposeful behavior occurs through the anticipation of sensory effects (see Hossner 2002). Therefore, the high quality of communication required here is subject to conditions that can have a critical impact on the players' cognition, anticipation, and comprehension processes, especially as concerns soccer training (see te Poel 1984). Such conditions include action-based versus positional orientation and the influence of coaches, parents, instructors, trainers, clubs, associations, fans, advisors, and the media. Consequently, the approach presented in this book is not only subject to a purpose-and-means relationship—take the Passing Puzzle® (see chapter 4.1), and success is yours!—but it is also linked to parameters in the training and continued training of soccer players that facilitate

- relationships between the acting people,
- long-term setup of a structure, and
- continuity and creating meaning.

(See also Hänsel/Baumgärtner 2014, pg. 37-62, on the conception of team cognitions.)

---

4   The interested reader can find further analyses and neurophysiological contexts of justification at McClelland et al. (1986) and Nitsch (1997).

Digression: Applicable here is a recent demand by the captain of the German national soccer team, Philipp Lahm (Frankfurter Allgemeine Zeitung, Nov. 7, 2013, 259, pg. 24). He demands a fixed position on the national team in the future, which the writer of the article, Christian Eichler, thinks is motivated by the "disloyalty of the coaches." What does he mean by that? Today's professional soccer instructors demand "versatility" from their players. For some players, this versatility can also become a "curse,[...]because coaches often love to move these players around while others are rewarded for being one-sided and are always allowed to play in their favorite position." (Frankfurter Allgemeine Zeitung 2013) What he surely did not consider here are a coach's methodological and didactic objectives:

1. The desire to continuously improve players. This is also true for world-class players. The methodological principle of variability, in this case playing in very different positions, represents a performance-enhancing instrument of choice.
2. To create a balance in his team's game, to make optimal dependability and variability in the course of a game, a season, and a tournament possible.

Looking at it this way, coaches aren't just "...interminably mobile Me, Incs"
(Frankfurter Allgemeine Zeitung 2013).

In addition, coincidence shouldn't be underestimated in pro soccer, because no soccer philosophy can guarantee success.

Memmert/Strauß, & Theweleit (2013, pg. 96) are even able to put an exact number to the coincidence contingent and refer to the current research results by Heuer (2012), Loy (2012), and Lames (1999):

Be it as it may, according to the above definition, coincidence plays a part in roughly 45% of all goals [...]Other results show that 35% of all touches have a coincident component."
From this, Memmert/Strauß & Theweleit (pg. 97) deduce the following for training and instruction:

"In contrast, truly good teams—the best example is FC Barcelona—try to avoid coincidental situations as much as possible. [...] The idea is to minimize coincidence to remain as independent as possible of the strange caprices of a soccer god. And you can look at it like this: roughly 55% of all goals are not random. Thus the greater part of a team's fortune still rests in its own feet."

Regarding the arguably best soccer team in the world at this time, FC Bayern Munich, José Mourinho, head coach of FC Chelsea London and winner of national titles with his various teams in Portugal, England, Italy, and Spain, characterizes outstanding teams as "[...]big teams with a big mindset and fantastic soccer-playing qualities." (2014, pg. 6).

All of this speaks for the optimal planning and management of training!

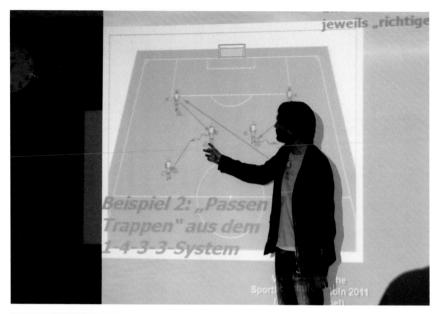

Preliminary theoretical game considerations help to develop optimal planning and management of soccer training! Here Hyballa and te Poel can be seen at a joint presentation in Cologne.

Hans-Dieter te Poel
German Sport University Cologne (Institut of Cognitive and Team / Racket Sport Research)

03

A PASS IS A PASS
IS A PASS?

03

A PASS IS A PASS IS A PASS?

> *"Having an orchestra with the ten best guitarists, but no pianist, is not a good thing."*
>
> (UEFA pro soccer instructor Manuel Pellegrini, Manchester City, in the *Frankfurter Allgemeine Zeitung*, Oct. 2, 2013, pg. 28)

When describing and analyzing passing play in soccer, it is often assumed that player A passes to player B. When player A's ball gets to player B, the coach is satisfied, but not if it's the other way around! Passing is much more than black-or-white thinking, as can be inferred from chapters 1 and 2. The complexity of the game fundamentally requires players to situationally and without impediment master many types of passes that should be practiced during training in the form of drills and games. And if a player still encounters a coach's particular playing "philosophy," as is the norm particularly in pro soccer, that can be expressed in practice and competition through quick switching play, pressing, long possession times, wrong-foot tactic on the wings[5], short or long passes, the expectation of the players is for diverse passes with many variations and combinations that have been acquired during professional training for a professional soccer player. If this is not the case, players are faced with a dilemma: Do they "pass" according to the coach's playing philosophy, or not, and is the player able to, for instance, effectively adjust to multiple coach or club changes?

---

5   *This means that a left foot plays on the right and a right foot plays on the left side (examples are Philipp Lahm on defense and Arjen Robben on offense). This tactic allows the player a certain amount of unpredictability. He can quickly pull to the inside or is better able to play with the 6/8/10 because he is able to use his preferred passing foot. Coaches and instructors can also use the wrong-foot tactic in youth soccer as a tool to practice playing with both feet.*

When comparing a coach's (or club's) different possible playing philosophies—for instance the FC Barcelona training school La Masia—with a painter's different paint cans, it quickly becomes apparent that all of his color philosophies are based on the *primary colors* and many mixed colors. In this respect, the painter does not ask himself, "How do I paint my picture?" but rather, "What do I need to do to depict a topic or problem that is important to me?" He will then supplement the same with the chronological division of his actions and work: "When do I have to mix or apply this or that color?" Only then will he subsequently move on to the "How to," meaning the painting technique. If we apply this example to soccer training, it becomes clear that for ambitious soccer training a purely technical approach ("How to pass?") with an exclusively methodological-didactic reasoning falls way short. Meanwhile there is much empirical evidence from game sports research that unequivocally documents implicit and explicit appropriation processes in games work autonomously and at the same time in cooperative or competitive interaction (see Hoffman 1993; Roth 1996; Szymanski 1997: Raab 2000; Memmert 2003). According to Furley and Memmert (2013), the pass "How to" turns into a "Whom should I pass to?"

"The more options, the more attentional guidance from working memory."

During training, the players' decision-making processes should be shaped in such a way that top-down and bottom-up processes are made possible through structuring of the learning situation. In this context, bottom-up processes apply to training the ability to differentiate relevant from non-relevant situational characteristics with instructions to the information sources. Top-down processes involve the player's options for developing the appropriate methods for structuring the situation, including instructions that help resolve situations in a game or at practice (Furley and Memmert 2013, pg. 204-205).

Hence it is the formal training (meaning, *our training*) that helps develop a diverse and varied repertoire of strategies, skills, and decision-making heuristic techniques in the player so that he is then able to use different situation-specific decision-making techniques to solve the task (e.g., in the sense of an overall playing philosophy) (see

Raab 2000). This makes the separation of motility and cognitions obsolete (see Memmert 2003, pg. 232).

Furthermore, empirical evidence exists, showing that familiar and stable action patterns (here with respect to the passing game in a broader sense) can be developed via training even in smaller clubs. So the desired precision and speed "[...] develops on its own, as long as the players can rely on their stable and jointly, over time, acquired action patterns." (Raadts 2009, pg. 262)

Thus a pass cannot be just a pass, which is argument for the interim solution that soccer training requirements should be chosen in such a way that

- the player is able to experience the requirement profile and the specific complexity of playing soccer,

"Because soccer is not always fun, beauty, joy; sometimes it is really rough and requires different abilities."

(The 100-time German national team player Bastian Schweinsteiger, FC Bayern Munich, in a kicker interview with Hartmann, O. & Wild, K., Oct. 14, 2013, pg. 10)

- "precipitousness" is checked via emotional control during passing, and
- the players' motivation, distribution, concentration, and teamwork (in the sense of educational perspectives and competencies) during training should be "kept up" with diverse, challenging, and cooperative tasks,

"Athletes in a promotion mode produce not only more adequate solutions, but also more original and flexible solutions in sport-specific divergent thinking tasks than athletes in prevention mode... We are able to show that the generation of creative solutions can be optimized through changing the athletes' motivational states."

(Memmert/Hüttermann & Orliczek 2013)

- varied divergent (creative thinking ability) and convergent (if-then relationships) can be developed,

- the players' organism can prevent future informational overload (by learning with emotional control) through reinforcement ("I did that well!") and differentiation ("Next time I need to resolve the situation with a different type of pass!"), and
- make sure that the structuring of relevant information via explicit methods particularly in the training of U-teams are subject to prior gathering of extensive action experience .[6]

Furthermore, direct and indirect factors that impact training and instruction must be taken into account:

- endogenic biological growth and maturing processes
- informational stimuli (motor coordination, perceptive, cognitive), different from physical adaptations (fitness training in general) because physical adaptations can trigger learning processes that take place suddenly (versus additive and successive learning processes) and are organ specific, leading to relatively stable results (see Hossner 2005, pg. 116-131)
- historic and cultural parameters
- social, environmental factors and personality factors

In club practice, those direct and indirect factors determine the desired regular participation in passing. "A pass is not just a pass" therefore means that passing practice places very high demands on target and structural planning in terms of overall training design and management (long-term, mid-term, short-term), because many (and mostly occurring simultaneously) performance factors are activated during the training process. Due to the limited publication, the if and when of integrating chosen topics into active training within the scope of the very complex control via regulatory circuit or block model or a synergetic approach cannot be addressed here. Additional specific methodological considerations and recommendations for training can be found in chapter 4.5.

---

6 We refer the interested reader to the following continuative literature: Aebli (1980; 1981) and Wahl (1991; 2006).

04

THE PASSING GAME IS A PREREQUISITE FOR GOOD SOCCER

THE PASSING GAME IS A PREREQUISITE FOR GOOD SOCCER:

THE HYBALLA/TE POEL PASSING PUZZLE IQ®

> When Steve Evets asked the famous French soccer player Eric Cantona (formerly of Manchester United) what the most wonderful moment of his career was, he replied: "It was a pass."
>
> (Dialogue from the film *Looking for Eric*, 2009, directed by Ken Loach).

Chapters 1, 2, and 3 emphasize the validity of this chapter's title.

Everyday training experience tells us that soccer training should not be overloaded with too much content and too many methods. This requires set priorities that include other performance factors, such as technique, tactics, fitness, psyche (mindset and creativity), and intelligence, and a playing philosophy in training; these are then coached by the coach or team instructor in individual, group, and team practices, according to the 11v11, 9v9, and 7v7 match requirements.

Working as a coach or instructor, it makes sense to visualize different game situations in which "my and the opposing team's" passing game, with its pre-, main-, and post-actions, play a role to find the right fit. When looking at these game situations, it is usually obvious right away that the classic style of two-footed, precise passing with the inside foot to utilize the field's depth and width is still of foremost importance.

But at second glance it also becomes clear that many game situations occur in

which that does not happen, and other types of passes that are tools for team-oriented passing become more important—for example, the up-and-over pass or the lob pass (see fig. 2 of the Passing Puzzle®).

Like the director of the German Soccer Association (DFB) instructor training program, Frank Wormuth (2011, pg. 43-47), we believe that as many different types of passes as possible should be practiced two-footed and under competition-like conditions again and again in practice, particularly in the targeted and effective promotion of youth training and where playing philosophies are subject to permanent change (all-rounder vs. specialist).

> *"As early as 2007, Joachim Löw made these same arguments regarding our current standings in international soccer. A lack of basic skills: tackles, passing speed, precision, carrying the ball, running speed – elementary, trainable factors!"*
>
> *Löw: "In really big teams these skills are highly developed. The players rarely make mistakes during simple actions!"*
>
> (Wormuth 2011, pg. 45).

For this reason Frank Wormuth demands detail work, as do we, and with respect to training holds firm to the following assertion:

"When individual subcomponents don't work, the entire game doesn't work."
(Wormuth 2011, pg. 46).

The following Passing Puzzle® contributes to the ever-present quest for the highest quality passes. But it always includes attention to the time factor in the selection of drills and forms of play and the self-referential communal exchange (as in a team or group), because: "Every action in its structure is co-determined by previous and anticipated actions [...]. The isolated contemplation of an individual action in its present moment is therefore not sufficient [...]." (Nitsch 2004, pg. 14.) Having the players experience game and practice plays an important role in the desired positive development of fast, precise, variable, and creative passing play *as a group*.

4.1   WHY A PASSING PUZZLE®?

> *"Barça makes the game as simple as possible, breaks it down into its components, the basic parts of soccer, the finely-tuned interplay between ball and legs – an infinite number of short, incisive passes played at the right moment, at the right speed, with the right spin, to the correct foot, to the correct side of the foot. And all of this embedded in the collective movements of a swarm in which each individual always maintains the right distance to all the rest."*
> (Christian Eichler, *Frankfurter Allgemeine Zeitung*, Sunday edition, n.y. and n.pg.).

The *etymological dictionary* of the German language defines the term puzzle as "a picture composed of individual parts" (Kluge 1999, pg. 656). However, the origin of the term is not clarified. Today it has resurfaced in modern English and is defined as "confusion" (Kluge 1999). In Germany its colloquial use is in connection with puzzles and in this context is synonymous with "game of patience" (Duden 1996, pg. 597).

But what does the puzzle have to do with the selected Passing Puzzle®? If one takes a closer look at FC Barcelona's Tiqui-Taca, it is very similar to a *game of patience* with at times *confusing* pass combinations, consisting of individual components of *one-touch passes* combined with *triangle passes, angle, and give-and-go passes*. These are practiced in competition-like conditions. This way, the players can act in tight spaces without losing possession according to their own or the opponent's game plan to practice wearing the opponent down, resting while in possession, or preparing to switch play or make a run. [7]

The situation is the question, the move (here the types of passes) is the answer.

---

7   *Descriptions and practice-oriented explanations of the names of the different types of passes (puzzles) and performance factors can be found in the practical section of the book (chapter 4.3).*

Linking the individual types of passes (the "details" = puzzles; fig. 3 with the puzzle's bottom transparency) with tactical aspects ("What is my/our game plan, and how do I implement it?") is logical and plausible because:

The higher the quality of the individual and team (coordinated) solution possibilities (in the sense of effective behavioral measures), the higher the level of play!

Terms are designed to help the coach or instructor make the situational coaching of drills or variations of plays easier for the players in practice and games with the help of soccer-specific, easy-to-understand verbal images and codes (e.g., the "last second pass"). This presupposes that the coach or instructor thoroughly discusses the coaching content and methods with the players and clearly explains the necessity of these specific agreements.

Therefore, this book fulfills a pivotal requirement of the DFB's soccer instructor training: "Training technique from a tactical point of view," and "Coaching is key!" (Wormuth 2011, pg. 46; also see chapter 4.5). But how? The following could be considered examples of situational coaching:

- *"No opponent in back? Crank it up!"*

- *"Opponent in back? One-touch pass!"*

- *"Behind the opponent? Pre-action: Get out of the cover shadow!"*

- *"Pass into space? Post-action: Go with the ball!"*

- *"Tight space, opponent presses? Tiqui-Taca, give-and-go, and bounce pass, or tight triangle passes!"*

- *"Playing out of the tight space"? Deep and wide switch passes!"*

As already emphasized in chapter 1, *situational coaching* cannot be limited to just evaluating solutions that are based on the "if-then rule," because most often these would result in "do it right/better one way or another" directions from the coach. Group-based action structures as they genuinely occur in a complex passing game also develop in the form of automatic, but (highly) intelligent, comprehension processes, so the player(s) can resolve the conditions they perceive as very demanding (e.g., enormous stress during competitions and new and complicated tasks) with precision, speed, variability, and appropriateness.

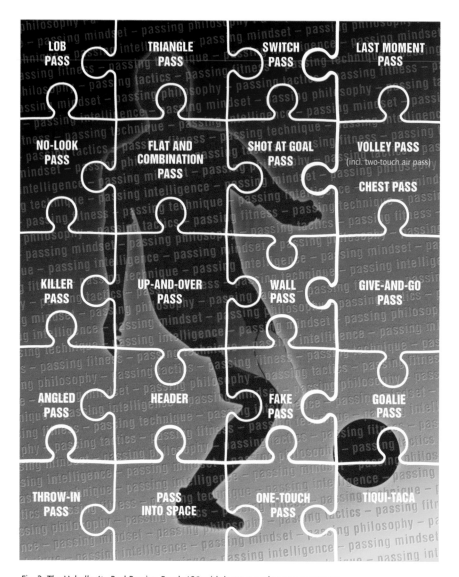

Fig. 2: The Hyballa/te Poel Passing Puzzle IQ® with bottom and top transparency

The *entire puzzle* represents the game (the picture) from which the individual pieces (the details) are derived as puzzles after intensive video analyses (see fig. 2).[8] This was the motivation for the choice of the conceptual pair Passing Puzzle®.

Fig. 2 shows the 20 selected puzzles in their entirety as the *top transparency* on top of the *bottom transparency* (see fig. 3), consisting of important performance-determining factors in the competitive soccer game.

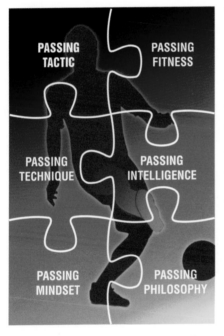

Fig. 3: The bottom transparency of the Hyballa/te Poel Passing Puzzle®

Whether regional league or top-level international soccer, the coach or instructor can choose from the 20 puzzles to coach his team or group and adopt the appropriate content (see chapter 4.3). He can also change the chosen terminology and adapt it to his team's or group's coaching language.

With the exception of *set pieces*, the pass never stands apart from the center of practice and playing activity. Thus the killer pass, which is usually played as a last ball into the opponent's danger zone, can also be interpreted as an up-and-over pass. The difference between both types of passes is primarily the chief technical characteristic of the pass: The killer pass is often played as a flat pass, or a *pass into the seam*, and the up-and-over pass, as the name implies, technically is played as a waist-high or high lob or switch pass. Another example of the close connections between the individual puzzles is the *third man play*. In practice or a game this requires a triangle

---

8   *In modern soccer the misdirected pass is still often used deliberately for passes into space. Often the reason for this in a game is to a) allow the opponent to get the ball and then run directly at him and press him, b) speculate on the second ball (e.g., after a defensive header), or c) to misdirect the ball into the opposing corner to buy time just before the end of a game. This special form of play is not subsequently included in the puzzle. The puzzles in fig. 2 and 3 are registered trademarks (®).*

pass, combination pass, or a delayed wall pass. To us coaches and instructors, the reason for this is obvious: We need options for solutions, puzzles, for playing in tight spaces, and we should practice these regularly!

If we pursue this train of thought further, to continue this combination the players will use one-touch passes and passes into space because this may be the only way for them to outplay the seemingly well-organized opponent. They must act as quickly as possible in time and space. Thus, nothing is separate in practice and game: The 20 selected passes (puzzles) are pieces of a picture we call a competitive game. They can be integrated and combined without constraint. The IQ (*passing intelligence*) is the desired playing creativity that coaches, instructors, and trainers should exhibit while using the Passing Puzzle®.[9]

> *"But in top-level soccer minor details that mostly go unnoticed from the outside, often determine victory and defeat. It is all about thinking and acting quickly. I find the mastering of these minor details fascinating."*
>
> (The 100-time German national team player Bastian Schweinsteiger, FC Bayern Munich, in a *kicker* interview with Hartmann, O. & Wild, K., Oct. 14, 2013, pg. 11).

Figure 2 shows *passing intelligence* on the bottom transparency. The abbreviation IQ does not mean an ascertainable intellectual but rather a pointed characterization of intelligent learning processes through training, playing, and coaching in soccer, in which the players, with the aid of the passing game, relate to each other competitively and learn to correctly read the ideas of their teammates and opponents (see chapter 2 and especially Guilford [1967] on human intelligence).

---

9   Memmert and Roth (2003) differentiate from Guilford (1967) between two separate cognitive thinking mechanisms for game sports training and learning, based on structural similarity: 1. Tactical playing intelligence (convergent tactical thinking in terms of finding the best solution) and 2. tactical creativity (divergent tactical thinking to generate many solutions to problems in specific game situations, that can be seen as appropriate as well as original and surprising (see specifically Memmert 2012a, pg. 38-49). "No, I only listened to my intuition. To me it is important to keep the element of surprise. Everyone always says: Robben goes inside and takes a shot with the left. But it still always works. But sometimes I also go outside and cross. Most important is: Be unpredictable" (Arjen Robben, FC Bayern Munich and Netherlands national team from an interview with Christian Eichler for the Frankfurter Allgemeine Zeitung, Nov. 1, 2013, 254, pg. 30).

But the Passing Puzzle® would not be complete in some important ways concerning the complex transparency of our competitive soccer game if other performance-determining factors that should not be missed by the coach or instructor's "passing eye" during practice, and especially practice planning, were not included: *passing mindset, passing fitness, passing philosophy* (see fig. 3; chapter 4.3, 4.4, and 4.5):

> *"An outstanding soccer talent who thinks that everything will just come to him will definitely be passed up by those with less talent, but lots of self-motivation and a tough mindset. And mental toughness is often the decisive difference."*
>
> (Norbert Elgert, U19 coach of FC Schalke 04 and Coach of the Year 2014, in a *kicker* interview with Müller, T., April 28, 2014, pg. 79).

- *Passing mindset* is a way of thinking that is often openly critical of the importance of passing in competitive play—particularly in professional soccer training—and that displays the following basic attitude:

> *"...maximum commitment to training and maximum regeneration. [...] Being able to make it as a professional requires lots of effort, and even more sacrifice. I said: If you want to enjoy Berlin, find a different job!"*
>
> (Jos Luhukay, former head coach at Hertha BSC, from a *kicker* interview with Röser, U. & Beer, J.-J., Sept. 9, 2013, pg. 13.)

The Dutch world-class coach Bert van Marwijk, vice world champion with the Netherlands national team, characterizes the significance of mindset in professional soccer with the following words: "What matters is a good presence on the field. We must project the mindset of a team that wants to win." (Quoted from a German press release in the *Neue Nassauische Presse*, Feb. 1, 2014, pg. 7). With respect to today's generation of professional soccer players, he makes the following observation in the same press release: "Nowadays hardly any team has individuals who radiate the attitude: This far and no further! in one-on-one duels." Bert van Marwijk attributes this to the increased media consumption.

From the perspective of a world-class player it sounds like this:

> *"There is no better recipe in soccer than work and faith in oneself. This combination opens doors for anyone, everywhere. Young players need to internalize this. Of course there are players who possess fantastic abilities. But they, too, have to work. It just isn't that obvious. And sometimes there are younger players who don't see that. They think you either have it, or you don't. Wrong! You have to prove yourself every day, even in practice. To the coach, the teammates, but especially to yourself!"*
>
> (Dante, player with FC Bayern Munich and the Brazilian national team, in a *kicker* interview with M. Zitouni, Dec. 2, 2013, pg. 13).

But players also have to be ready to think quickly: 1. Pre-action: Be at the ready. Where am I on the field? Where can I help out? 2. Main action: Controlling the ball and passing, or one-touch (relative to the topic)? 3. Post-action: Moving, getting open, feinting, stopping, etc.

Where the opponent's *passing mindset* is concerned, a high degree of emotional control and frustration tolerance must be practiced when practicing defensive play:

> *"... not getting frustrated when we don't have a lot of possession."*
>
> Head coach Christian Streich of Budesliga team SC Freiburg regarding opponent FC Bayern Munich, quoted in the *Frankfurter Neue Presse*, Aug. 27, 2013, pg. 7)

Behavior plays a significant role, particularly in the practical work with youth players.

Recent findings from motivation and stress research now show that "... a person's stress response is influenced by the interaction between its motivational focus of winning or avoiding losing and the environment" (Schwab 2013, iii). To what extent the coach or instructor must therefore plan and design the scope of passing training in the future so that it corresponds to the player's regulatory focus and thus enables him to achieve a higher performance is still unresolved, but it is of great interest in regards to goal-driven performance optimization. However, we are unable to further address additional current findings on motivation and stress at this point (see Schwab 2013 and chapter 4.5).

> *"No matter what you have achieved, you always have to keep both feet on the ground. To me character and mindset are what is most important in soccer."*
> (Arjen Robben, player for FC Bayern Munich and the Netherlands national team, from an interview with Christian Eichler in the *Frankfurter Allgemeine Zeitung*, Nov. 1, 2013, 254, pg. 30).

> *"I like to put the team under a healthy amount of pressure. I have learned that every person performs better with a little pressure. I also put a certain amount of pressure on myself. But it always has to be realistic."*
> (Bert van Marwijk, former head coach at Hamburg Sports Club and coach for the Netherlands national team, from an interview with Sebastian Wolff in *kicker* interview, Nov. 18, 2013, 94, pg. 43).

After losing several games in the Bundesliga and the Champions League first leg game against Real Madrid in 2014, there was discussion in the national and international press about whether the "possession soccer" played by FC Bayern Munich under head coach Pep Guardiola would be enough to compensate for form fluctuations and mood swings in a top-level team:

> *"Guardiola views success as a question of style. German soccer views success as a question of mind over matter. [...] FC Bayern Munich doesn't need Germany, they need the German spirit."*
> (Christian Eichler in the *Frankfurter Allgemeine Zeitung*, April 28, 2014, No. 98, pg. 23).

This example from the game of the current and probably most successful soccer club team in the world also illustrates that the force of will, the *mindset*, is a mode of behavior that many observers in very successful German soccer consider an important part of soccer culture and a kind of virtuous trait that can help to correct performance fluctuations and successfully engage teams in competitive games "on a par" with "...

full throttle, passion, and heart" (Philipp Lahm) (see Christian Eichler in the *Frankfurter Allgemeine Zeitung*, April 28, 2014, No. 98, pg. 23).

- *Passing fitness* lays the *physical foundation* for the implementation of the Passing Puzzle®. Studies on players' position and speed-related data in professional soccer clearly show that the players' total running distances have greatly increased in recent years and are significantly influenced ($p = 0.001$) by the playing position. In this context, the outside midfielders and fullbacks cover 10,345 ($\pm$ 686) m and 10,035 ($\pm$ 477) m during 90 minutes of playing time (see Siegle et al. 2012, pg. 280).

This is also true for the running intensities in which the two outside midfielders and forwards significantly differ from other playing positions with maximum values of 167 ($\pm$ 87) and 164 ($\pm$ 69) sprints (see Siegle et al. 2012, pg. 281). Therefore, passing fitness should be included in the puzzle picture, and in addition to the main passing action, pre- and post-action terminology are introduced in the following examples of game situations each coach and instructor must consider during practice (see also chapter 4.2).

The *passing philosophy* refers to the coach or instructor's *soccer IQ* and *level of knowledge*:

- Which puzzle is particularly important to the players and me?
- Where and when do we have to play with patience?
- Where and when do we need to create angles in the game?
- Get moving, dribble, pick up the pace!
- When to go wide, when to go deep? What does the current situation demand?
- Return pass to the goalie, then keep creating passing opportunities for the goalie! Counterexample: A goal scored against Germany after a return pass to Marc-André ter Stegen against the US in 2013. Elements like these sometimes become symbolic of the competitive play of one's own team (e.g., steady buildup vs. fast counters). The individual playing philosophies should be compatible with those of the club because in difficult athletic situations the coach's or instructor's authenticity and

the advancement of the club are always subject to negotiation. Ideally a club has a consistent *passing philosophy* (see chapter 4.4).

This means that the players are able to understand (and thus more effectively learn) the *passing philosophy*, especially in youth soccer.

During competitive play the coach, instructor, and player are able to see in real time what the pass picture looks like. The target performance comparison (including situational peculiarities) enables the coach or instructor to constantly continue to "paint" the picture or to discard it and start a new picture. The colors for this, in keeping with the imagery in chapter 3, can be found in the well-stocked shelves at the hardware store (see fig. 2). Not only are there 20 different colors (puzzles) available for sale and use here, but also six examples of possible "styles" (key performance elements) that can be freely combined by the coach (bottom transparency; see fig. 3). This approach is put into practice in subchapter 4.3.1 with the assignment of "styles" to the 20 puzzles and the many practice and teaching methods.

"It's a puzzle and you have to put the pieces together, and that's what I did this week!"

(Response by Swiss top tennis pro Stanislas Wawrinka at the ATP finals of the world's best male tennis players, to the question, why he has only become one of the four best players in the world at age 28. Quoted in the *Frankfurter Allgemeine Zeitung*, Nov. 11, 2013, pg. 15).

4.2 WHY A PASSING GRID?

"Their passes became more precise and the positions became more and more difficult to figure out, the running paths practically flowed into each other without requiring any commands."

(Sports writer Richard Leipold in his article "The Bavarians' paths are bottomless," *Frankfurter Allgemeine Zeitung*, Sept. 23, 2013, pg. 15).

Since the days of Johan Cruijff, Louis van Gaal, and Pep Guardiola we have learned that soccer on the field is always about areas that must be manned in order to be able to promptly press, surround, or put pressure on the ball (cover the field). In this regard the distances of the players to each other are extremely important, and all players must be ready to actively play (see Hyballa and te Poel 2013, pg. 78-79). For example, if one plays in a 1-4-3-3 formation there are occasionally six lines on the field in which the distances between players should be 5 and 10 m (see fig 4 with dot, No. 10, in front).

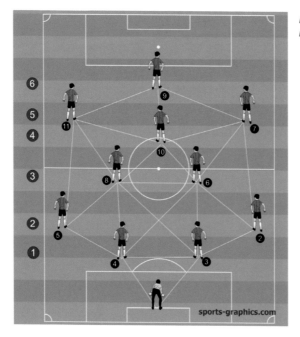

Fig. 4: Exemplary connecting lines in a 1-4-3-3 formation

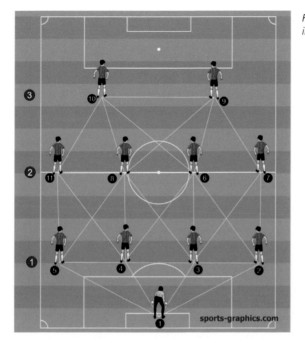

Fig. 5: Exemplary connection lines in a 1-4-4-2 formation

The result is that players use specific running, passing, and dribbling paths during offense and defense. By contrast, in a 1-4-4-2 formation with a *flat four*, there are only three or four lines on the field (see Hyballa and te Poel 2013, pg. 78) that create a different geometry on the field and involve different action patterns during offense and defense (covering space) (see fig. 5 with a flat four).

Like Pep Guardiola, we also believe that soccer fitness and the mental readiness for everyone defends, everyone attacks can also be practiced in a limited space with lines and zones: "Often Guardiola only plays in one half of the field. The players are supposed to get used to tight spaces. This half is often divided into 16 squares on which the players spread out. There they hold their positions until the playing direction of the ball shows them, which square to move to next. [...] That is why he [Guardiola] mixes chaos with order, street soccer with drafting table soccer in his practices." (Schulze-Marmeling, 2013, pg. 102)

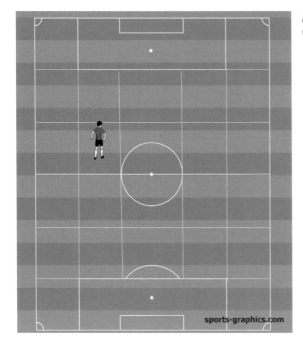

Fig. 6: From regulatory framework with line network (raster) to grid

sports-graphics.com

Transferring this idea to a whole playing field (see fig. 6) creates a positional game in zones in which the player is able to intensively practice his positions: "What can I do, and what can I not yet do?" Corresponding tasks will let this structure help the player feel like a fish in water, who knows his terrain and in it learns to pass with precision, speed, and creativity.

The examples show that the structure of grids the authors planned represents a regulatory framework for passing practice that can create the direct link to competitive play (and thereby the performance-determining factors) (see fig. 3). On the practice field the grids look like an array of dots (cones) (see fig. 6 with 30 points of contact and 20 fields). The coach or instructor organizes them in such a way that certain temporal and spatial distances can be bridged within the scope of the players' actions.

Of course the passes practiced between the individual cones are not straight and level only because this would not correspond to many game situations, such as switch passes with spin. Considering this perspective, the grid can also be thought of as a *dynamic net* from the player's point of view. This means movable intersections formed by the players near the cones. This network structure consists of several *independent* levels or subnets:

- the *tangible* level: the ball and its condition and that of the playing field
- the *informational* level: the flow of information, the purpose of plays (deliberate or automatic), and the form of the day
- the *social* level: sympathies and antipathies, good vs. bad cooperation partners, kindness vs. resentment, and spectator support

The positions of the cones in relation to each other reflect the purpose of the particular drill and thereby represent the basic information that characterizes the respective grid. To the observer this provides a pattern (with a distinctive design, see fig. 4 and 5). This is intended to help the players learn, or rather improve, their basic ability to classify in the sense of the Puzzle IQ.

They learn this in practice in the form of a grid taken directly from the players' point of view and do not have to additionally transfer the information that is described, recognized, analyzed, and interpreted, as is necessary with a simple video analysis from a bird's-eye view. Additional advantages of the grid for practical training include

- predictable practice and instruction;
- quick and easy setup;
- ability to quickly guide attention;
- position-specificity and team building (figuratively sport-specificity/demand profile);
- variable emphasis on focus areas in practice/instruction;
- targeted coaching (coach/instructor-player, player-coach/instructor, player-player);
- individual and group-specific training and instruction;
- dovetailing technique and tactics;
- developing a passing and playing philosophy by simplifying (manageable space);
- quick transfer of video analysis into grids;

- quickly adapting to the opponent with the help of grids;
- quick and simple options for linking different passes with the dribbling and shooting techniques; and
- simple accentuation of pre- and post-action via grids (distances should be made quick and variable) based on the motto: "Doing the dirty work!"

The grids will precede the forms of play and are no substitute for spontaneous action processes.

4.2.1 THE 3-ACTION SYSTEM

The grid can also help to thoroughly train the pre- and post-actions (post-play is pre-play—and vice versa!) with running drills like offering support and getting open. Training these actions is extremely important. Photos 1, 2, and 3 show these effective and basic elements.

Photo 1: Pre-action: Getting away from the opponent, but maintaining eye contact. (Photo: philippka sportverlag)

Photo 2: Main action: Precise push pass with the foot away from the opponent and with eye contact. (Photo: philippka sportverlag)

Photo 3: Post-action: Take-off. Getting open, keeping eye contact, and possibly regaining possession. (Photo: philippka sportverlag)

When the individual players are running, the player who is not in possession or has just passed the ball plays the crucial role: Will he carry out a post-action, or will he try to retake possession with a skilled pre-action? At times this requires a major physical commitment by the player, but at the same time it also places major demands on his cognitive ability (read situations), anticipation ability, cooperation ability, creativity, and decision-making ability, because: "After the ball is before the ball!"

In most cases coaches and instructors demand *intelligent running* from their players. But what does that mean? Different age groups run differently. For example, children run until they can't run anymore. Juniors often run in closed spaces on the field but will also expertly let the ball go. Pros move intelligently in open spaces, large or small, that can emerge when ball movement is precise and quick.

But how does one practice *intelligent running*? Many teams practice one-touch soccer in which they focus on the particular passing quality that the coaches are teaching: very good, play hard passes; stay precise and keep possession; not so many turns, take out the step, keep the ball on the ground, only play flat passes to the foot or into space, etc. Taking a look at the game situation, a player can usually keep possession when, in addition to passing play, two other actions take place: *the pre-action and the post-action* (see photos 1 and 3). Both actions take place at a certain speed and with a tactical focus. When looking at and practicing the passing quality separately, the competitive aspect is missing. With respect to teamwork in general adhere to the words by former Netherlands national team player Arnold Mühren:

> *"It is a thinking game. It is not about running all over the field and slogging away, although it does of course require hard work."*
> (In *Winner*, 2008, pg. 194).

What does Mühren mean by that?

- When the coach or instructor calls for movement in practice, he is not just asking the players to run back and forth, but is also looking for purposeful running or sprinting into appropriate spaces on the field to lay the foundation for quick short passing sequences.

- Outstanding teams often have possession because, in addition to their superior passing quality, they carry out lightning-fast actions with the ball (e.g., by immediately dribbling into open space) or close to the ball (e.g., with the intention of making space for a third player or a wall pass).

Reaching the level outlined by the coach requires the players to have a wealth of experience and *quality*. Both factors can already be observed in many younger players in top international leagues who have learned early on to play the game with lots of *brains*, meaning quickly getting out of the cover shadow, quickly sprinting away from and to the ball to free up a teammate, and playing *with heart* (i.e., with fighting capacity, dedication, running ability). Therefore, it will remain a coach's or instructor's main challenge to improve or optimize the pre- and post-action quality through appropriate coaching—here in the form of the passing grid. The players' inspiration is referred to by the generic term *EXTRA WORK*, or in soccer language also called and understood as overtime, extra shift, dirty work, intelligent work, and physical work. Regardless of which generic term the coach or instructor and players choose, it should help the team experience and learn that, for instance, the desire for successful and motivating combination play involves playing short and flat passes that entail EXTRA WORK in practices and games.

The mere pass from A to B is out! For us coaches and instructors this means: When practicing passing, don't just look at the pass but also pay attention to and coach the without-pass actions" before and after the pass. The players' log will have an entry: Mental and physical disconnect not allowed!" "Always stay tuned in!"

The different accentuations in the form of grids allow the coach or instructor to independently plan and implement soccer-specific fitness training paired with different types of passes and other focal points from the lowest to the highest playing level (see fig. 2 and 3). Thus the grid presents an *additional means* for integrating athletic training into soccer training without lots of additional practice time, equipment, space requirements, and external experts.

In retrospect our own training and teaching practice has showed us that forms of play and continuous drills in which players are merely positioned at corresponding cones teaches orientation behavior in a fixed space. But to prevent players from developing static and at times lackluster behavior—behavior coaches and instructors are well aware of—do not continuously use the fixed cone markers in the grid to limit how the players feel for the space.

What does this look like in the field?

- First use grids with cones and practice the different passing sequences (puzzles) several times in slow motion.
- Remove all or many of the cones and explain the task to the players one more time; then let them practice freely.

Usually the running, playing, and ball speeds of players who associate cones with constraint and restriction show very little reference to competitive play.

"Players want to be encouraged and challenged!"

The following quote by Dante, fullback for FC Bayern Munich and player on the Brazilian national team, from a kicker interview with M. Zitouni, Dec. 2, 2013, pg. 12, supports this assertion:

"Lucien Favre showed me how to simplify my game, and he was tactically very strong. Positional play and running paths, those were his forte. On the other hand, I credit Heynckes with the great composure in my game. With him I became more certain in my buildup. He taught me to be incredibly calm at the ball. He also was a coach who believed that there is room for improvement even at the highest level, and I liked that. And Pep is a blend of both."

A simple and extremely accessible description and explanation of the *sequence* and *purpose* of the grids associated with the EXTRA WORK prior to starting practices is therefore very important, especially for the players:

- Compatibility is more than good *passing technique*.
- Counterattack from the opponent, especially the pressure of time, space, and complexity, requires creating open spaces. Most often this can only be done with the appropriate running effort.
- Playing combination soccer until taking a shot always means: Keep the opponent moving!

> *When practicing passing, don't always just look at the pass. The EXTRA WORK is the magic word in coaching!*

In summary, the EXTRA WORK for planning practices and instruction can be explained with a *3-action system*:

1. *Pre-action:* The player runs to the ball or away from the ball or simply stops to get his teammate open. For youth players, in particular, who often just want to keep running (and who are often encouraged to do so to "fight"), this is a type of pre-action that has to be learned. This is also true with regard to taking the open position. By mastering this skill, players, especially in men's soccer, are able to let the ball do the work. The counterpart to this is the pre-action of taking a closed position. Often an opposing player can be blocked with the help of the closed position, thereby creating space for a teammate.

2. *Main action:* Here the authors differentiate between passing, dribbling, and creating space.
   a) Passing: The player executes a situation-appropriate pre-action, gets the ball, and plays it on as a one- or two-touch ball, respectively.
   b) Dribbling: The player sees the open space offered by the opponent and dribbles through it to push the opponent backward.

c) Creating space: The player executes the pre-action by running away from the ball. He thereby creates more space for his teammate, who is then able to pass the ball to a teammate relatively unchallenged, or allows the player in possession to dribble the ball through the now enlarged space.

3. *Post-action:* Since the reference point to the ball changes, the player who passed the ball should execute an action. One option would be the running-after action. This does not just mean running after one's own ball but rather is intended to create spaces to make the opponent run. As previously mentioned with regard to pre-action, stopping can also be an important post-action to provide secure positioning of the remaining defenders or to open up the space (and not run up).

The following fig. 7 shows the practical execution of the 3-action system with an example emphasizing post-action.

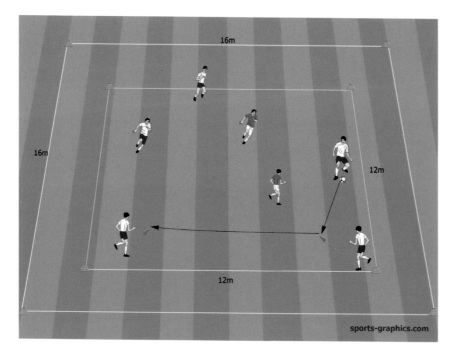

Fig. 7: 5 vs. 2 with post-action

Organization:

- 5v5 play in a space that is 14 x 14 m.
- Behind the 5v2 space, four other cones or markers are set up approximately 6 m apart.

Progression:

- The players play 5v2.
- The coaches or instructors specify any restrictions to ball contact.
- When a player passes the ball, he immediately has to sprint to one of the back cones (post-action) and then quickly back onto the field because the superior three-man situation should be exploited further.
- Playing times: 60-sec intervals and with modified tasks.

Coaching:

- The known post-action should not trigger hectic passing play!
- Avoid sloppy *square passes*!
- It is best to do a backward sprint to the cone: "Keep an eye on the game!"

Variations:

- One-touch play to decrease the distance.
- Set up cones on the field at a distance of 3 m (for *post-action*).
- Play with a *joker* who can move in the open space between the 5v2 and the cone for the post-action.
- The four cones for the *post-actions* are marked with two different colors. Red means a long running distance, and yellow means a short running distance. The coach determines the respective tasks.

4.3   THE INDIVIDUAL PUZZLE PIECES: IS IT ALL JUST A MATTER OF PASS TYPES?

"What is Messi: Midfielder or forward? Scorer or playmaker? The answer: He is all of those things in one; versatility personified. An all-rounder with universal abilities, blessed with gigantic skills."

(H.G. Klemm, Dec. 2, 2013, TOP SPEED. The New Kings of Soccer, in *kicker* 98, pg. 9)

Looking at the statements in previous chapters, the answer to the question posed in the chapter title would have to be no. It is therefore necessary that the individual puzzle pieces are hereinafter

- put into a concrete situational playing context,
- briefly outline the purpose of the training and instruction, and
- present effective and practical examples for the coach or instructor.

The question, How do I practice these puzzle pieces?, will be addressed separately in chapter 4.5. The structure of *organization, progression, coaching*, and *variations* chosen for the following chapters merely provides a rough pattern that is intended to provide the reader with particularly explicit, comprehensible, and productive material for the first steps into the *topics* (puzzle pieces). This training and instructional aid provided in advance, also called *advance organizer*, is meant to organize and structure the content, but it definitely does not discount the readers' or players' prior knowledge. The reader should then actively and independently use the *inventory of methods* (see chapter 4.5) like a building set or a color palette, based on his *individual experience* and his *needs*.

With respect to the (1) *technical* and (2) *tactical elements for (flat) passes*[10] we start with the following:

---

10   *A detailed description of the technical aspects of all other passes can be found in Bisanz/Gerisch (2013, pg. 332-363).*

(1) Technical elements:

- *Running at the ball:*
    - If possible, approach from behind the ball to be able to pass from an open position (see chapter 4.3.6).
    - Go into the ball when passing, meaning play the pass flat and with force.
- *Passing motion:*
    - The toe of the supporting leg points in the direction of the target.
    - *Flat pass:* The shooting leg follows through and gets big by using the supporting leg. *Coaching:* "Get up on the ball of the foot!", "Keep moving with the shot!", and "Don't root your supporting leg in the ground but take a very small hop forward!"
- *Passing techniques (flat pass):*
    - *Inside foot:* Frontal passes, short and mid-distance;
    - *Inside instep:* Diagonal passes
- *Outside instep:* See inside instep, whereby the shooting leg is in a lateral position to the target.

(2) Tactical elements:

- *Individually:*
    - Breaking away from the opponent or stepping out of the cover shadow and offering support in the gaps.
    - *Offering support for deep passes:* going into the gap (e.g., as a 6er, 9er).
    - *Offering support for return passes:* Having the gap in front to be able to immediately play a long ball through the gap.
    - *Offering support to the side:* facilitating diagonal balls.
    - Trying to get into the open position (see chapter 4.3.6) to immediately be able to play forward.
    - *Timing:* Break away early to receive a pass if the ball is still on its way to the teammate to allow the partner to make a direct pass.
- *Group tactics:*
    - *Wall pass,* playing with a third man, long ball with rebound.

- *Oblique/diagonal balls:* Play past the opponent diagonally to the front or back; the receiving player has a gap in front of him and can meet the ball half-open (see chapter 4.3.6).

In the following chapters, we also purposefully use mostly familiar soccer language, thereby anticipating an easier and quicker task-oriented transfer to practice and instruction. The figurative language chosen for the different types of passes has been used to date by coaches Hyballa and te Poel in their own practice as collective terminology. The intention is to establish an association between certain symbols, visual characters, and acoustical forms of words, and the objects that create different types of passes, and furthermore to support a team's communication process.

4.3.1 THE LOB PASS

"Ideal is when one is proactive, when one plays assertively, is dominant, is multi-faceted."

(The 100-time German national team player Bastian Schweinsteiger, FC Bayern Munich, in a *kicker* interview with O. Hartmann & K. Wild, Oct. 14, 2013, pg. 11).

In a competitive game, the *lob pass* is mostly needed when an opponent is positioned directly in front of the player in possession. The player with the ball urgently wants to pass to his teammate. He either needs to look for the 1v1, play via a third man, or lob the ball over the opponent. This is also called *chipping the ball* over the opponent. This situation is comparable to lobbing in a tennis match.

The following fig. 8 shows a simulated *lob pass* situation on the wing (in a 2v3 situation) taken form the Champions League game Arsenal London (here in white/ blue) against BV Borussia Dortmund 09, from Nov. 12, 2011, at a 0-0 score (action starts at 5:30 minutes of playing time).

Fig. 8: Lob pass from the Champions League game Arsenal London vs. BV Borussia Dortmund 09

But often the *lob pass* is also played when space in the game is very tight (e.g., near the opposing penalty area) and is then played as a *final pass* to catch the opposing central defenders off-guard. Zidane was a master of the *lob pass*, a technically ingenious passer.

EXAMPLES FOR PRACTICE AND INSTRUCTION

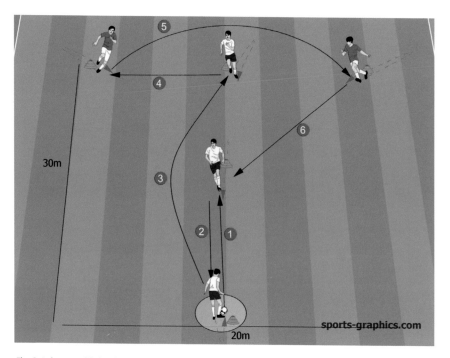

Fig. 9: Lob pass with five in the passing grid

Organization:

- Five cones are placed in an approximately 30-x-20-m space.
- A player positions at each cone so that the passing grid will be completed with 5 players.

Progression:

- A player passes the ball to the opposite player. This player allows the ball to rebound, and the first player lobs the ball over the second player to the third player, who stands opposite him about 15 m away.
- The third player plays the *lobbed* ball directly to the fourth player who stands to his side.
- He *lobs* the ball over the third player to the fifth player, who then passes the ball to the second player, thereby ending the exercise.

Coaching:

- Demand body tension from all players.
- Demand *two-footed* lobbing.
- The ball must be *lobbed* hard and with precision so a new play can be initiated.

Variations:

- Only practice the *lob* pass with a specific passing foot.
- Increase the distances and play the *lob pass* incisively to the teammate's head.
- Simulate game situations: Set up two passing grids next to each other and man them with a total of 10 players. Who finishes the exercise fastest (time, bonus points, etc.)?

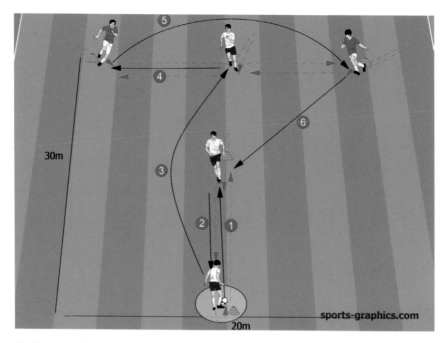

Fig. 10: Lob pass in a grid of five and position changes

Organization: See fig. 9.

Progression:

- See fig. 9, whereby the players in the circles switch positions with their opposites after the *lob pass*.
- After the *lob pass* all players play the ball with one touch ("Direct play!")

Coaching:

- Demand, *"Play and go!"*
- After the *lob pass* all players must orient themselves to the respective new space *(passing tactics)*.
- Don't put too much *spin* on the lob pass!

Variations:

- Increase the distances so that a player, for instance in the light-green circle, has to execute several *lob passes* at a time. He should always run after his own *lob pass*.

- In addition to passing from a closed position, the players also pass the ball to each other the ball from a *double-pass situation*.
- Add one goal with a goalie, and after the *lob pass*, end the complete action with a shot at goal.

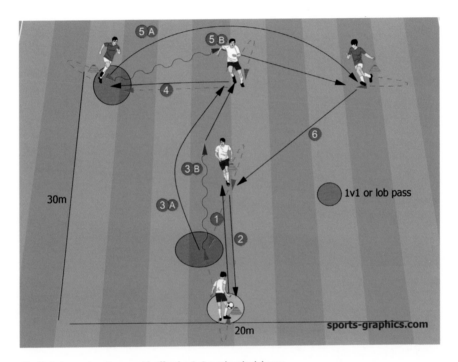

Fig. 11: Lob pass in a 5-man grid: offensive 1v1 or play the lob pass

Organization: See fig. 9

Progression:

- As in fig. 9, the player letting the ball rebound immediately becomes the defensive opponent.
- By doing this the player receiving the ball can decide if he wants to play offensive 1v1 or use the *lob pass*.
- Every player who used the *lob pass* immediately becomes the defensive opponent (long and short running paths).

Coaching:

- Demand speed and precision from the fast opponent.
- Encourage quick or delayed decisions[11] (offensive 1v1 or *lob pass*) (*passing tactics*).

Variations:

- Increase distances between players to prompt the player in possession to dribble.
- Decrease the distances between players so that the players only require one or two touches to make their decisions.
- Execute the *lob pass* with two touches. *Lob the ball into the air* with the first touch and play it away with the second touch.

Fig. 12: 4v4 plus 2 lob pass players

Organization:

- 4v4 at two big goals with goalies in a space that is 40 x 30 m.
- Two neutral players are added, making it 4v4 plus 2.

---

11   *Based on the pre-decision, pre-action, and post-action phase by Höhner (2005, pg.36)*

Progression:

- See Progression, Fig. 11
- The two neutral players are part of the team in possession. These two players can only play *lob passes* (*ground passes* are not allowed).

Coaching:

- Focus on quickly settling and controlling the ball in the 4v4.
- The neutral players must be able to determine if the *lob pass* should be played into space or to the teammate's foot.
- Play additional *lob passes* with the inside foot (*passing technique*).

Variations:

- Change the size of the playing field so that the *lob passes* can be played farther.
- The two neutral players play open soccer, whereby only the final assist before a shot can be a *lob pass*.
- The two neutral players are allowed to play *ground passes*, whereby the goal must be scored with a *lob pass*. The two neutral players can also score.

Fig. 13: 6v6 with goalie—lob passes instead of offensive 1v1

Organization:

- 12 players plus 2 goalies play open at two goals on a 55-x-30-m fields.

Progression:

- 6v6 with unlimited touches.
- The ball can be moved with a pass.
- No offensive 1v1 is played. The ball is played forward, and a *lob pass* must be used instead of the offensive 1v1.

Coaching:

- When the player in possession is pressured by the opposing players, he must quickly use the *lob pass*.
- The player without the ball should provoke the lob pass and skillfully start into the space to claim it (*passing technique*).
- If the player in possession is overwhelmed, he can also blindly play the ball into the space.

Variations:

- In the 6v6, the ball is only lobbed, and as soon as it hits the ground, offensive 1v1 action must follow.

- In the 6v6, only one mandatory touch is played. As soon as a player accepts the ball, he must pass it on with a *lob pass*.

- If a *lob pass* is played in the game the player who receives the ball must immediately take a shot at goal, making a quick or delayed decision (see Höhner, 2005, pg. 36).

4.3.2 THE TRIANGLE PASS

"The 'triangle' clearly shows the passing lines and the decisions the players make. The players recognize this later, in the game situation."
(Louis van Gaal, 2010, pg. 100).

Triangle passes are done with three players. This type of pass is based on the premise that the second player is aware of the third player to help speed up the game situation (and the game).

The three players involved do not always have to be positioned in a triangle. But here we point out that the *triangle formation* has the following advantages:

- deep passes
- wide passes (*passing technique*)

Triangle passes presuppose that the player with the ball is able to quickly read the game situation and possesses a solid *passing technique* to forward the ball unimpeded.

The player without the ball must anticipate when to start into the space or remain in his position to receive the third ball (*passing intelligence*).

This makes it apparent that a *triangle pass* is not just a *passing technique* (see Bisanz and Gerisch 2013, pg. 332-363), but it also includes What and How questions regarding tactical abilities and skills. The idea behind the triangle pass is this:

"Speed up the game or control it!"

The following fig. 14 shows a simulated *triangle pass* situation in conjunction with a *pass into space* (see chapter 4.3.16) in the opposing half, from the Champions League game FC Barcelona (here in red/white) against Manchester United (white/blue) from May 2011, with a 0-0 score (start of action at 9:57 min. of playing time).

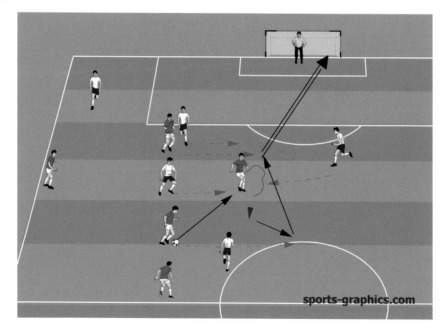

Fig. 14: Triangle pass in conjunction with pass into space from the Champions League game FC Barcelona vs. Manchester United

EXAMPLES FOR PRACTICE AND INSTRUCTION

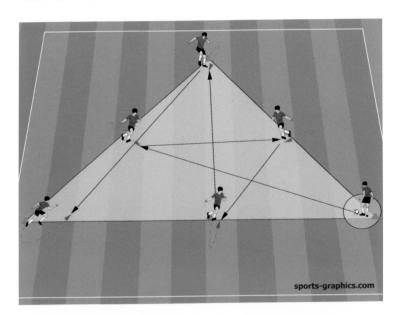

Fig. 15a: Triangle passes in a grid of six

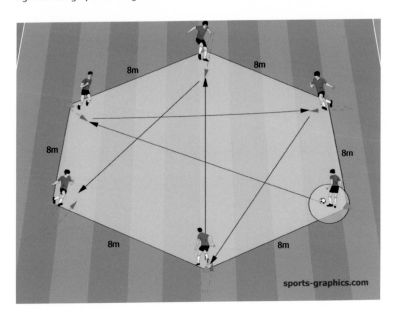

Fig. 15b: Triangle passes in a grid of six

Organization:

- Six cones are set up in the space so that the distance between the individual cones is approximately 8 m.
- The cones can be set up in triangle formations (see fig. 15a or 15b).

Progression:

- Each player positions himself at a cone.
- The players play with one ball and should keep the ball moving constantly in different triangle formations.
- No *square passes* are allowed.
- The ball can only be passed via the third player, so it is not played to where it was passed from.

Coaching:

- Before the player receives the ball, the player without the ball must decide where to pass it.
- Before the pass is played to the next row, the player in possession must turn with precision.
- "Focus on an incisive and quick *passing technique!*"

Variations:

- Only play with one touch.
- Only play with one or two touches.
- The ball can be played back. But subsequently it must be opened to the other side.

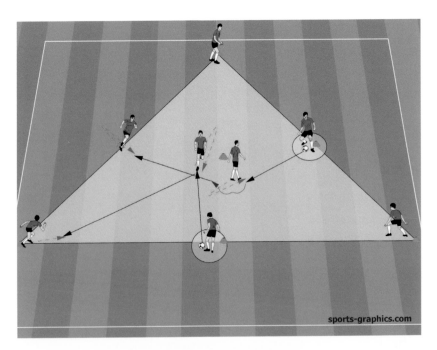

Fig. 16a: Grid with seven players and forward-turning action in the center

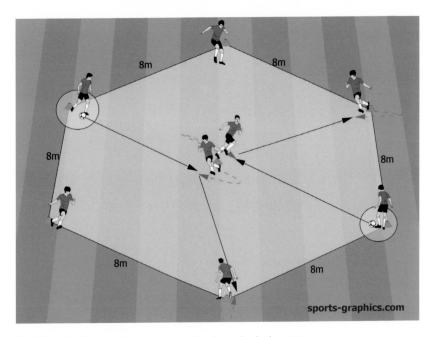

Fig. 16b: Grid with seven players and forward-turning action in the center

Organization:

- See Fig. 16a and 16b, whereby an additional cone and a player are positioned in the center of the space (central player). This results in two grids of seven with triangle formations.

Progression:

- The players look for the players in the center, who pass the ball on to another player.
- The ball can be passed to a player who stands in front of them, or they have to cut outside to speed up the ball.
- Practice with two balls.
- No player is allowed to remain at his cone, but instead must create space.

Coaching:

- The two central players must cut outside.
- The two balls in play cannot simultaneously be in the same half of a triangle.
- If the two balls in play travel too fast, ball speed must be reduced.

Variations:

- Practice with one ball and call specific passing and running lanes.
- Execute *triangle passes* with position changes.
- The coach determines the ball speed: sometimes slow Tiqui-Taca, sometimes quick opening passes (*passing philosophy*)

See fig. 16a and 16b: Grid with seven players without forward-turning actions in the center (no images).

Organization: See fig. 15a and 15b.

Progression:

- Both central players only act as *rebounders*[12] who let the ball *bounce* within their triangle formation.

---

12 *Letting the ball bounce or rebound is generally associated with the technique of one-touch play into all playing directions and is linked to the search for a new running path. The interested reader can find practical suggestions in Hyballa and te Poel (2013b, pg. 46).*

- The outside players, on the other hand, must use the ball to open up the space, meaning: "Play the ball to the other side, too!"
- This generates *triangle passes* that act as opening passes because the central players can only stay in the closed position.

Coaching:

- Play the opening pass vertically or diagonally with the appropriate speed (*passing mindset*).
- The central players play a slow ball in preparation to the opening *triangle pass*.

Variations:

- Practice with one ball.
- Add a large goal with a goalie. In this variation, the shot at goal should be integrated as a finish (i.e., final action).
- If the coach or instructor wants to set up the triangle with the central players, the *lob pass* can be interspersed.

See fig. 16a and 16b: Grid with seven players in a tight or opening space.

Organization: See fig. 16a and 16b.

Progression:

- See fig. 16a and 16b. The players without the ball must decide if they want to stand in front of the cone (= tight space) that will be the target of lots of one-touch actions, or be ready to receive the ball behind the cone (= wide space) to engage in a game-like 1v1 (cone) with the ball at the foot and then play the *triangle pass.*
- Start the exercise with just one ball.

Coaching:

- The player who stands in the wide space without the ball must start straight forward with the first touch.
- The player who stands in the tight space without the ball must play an incisive (precise) *flat pass* with one touch and immediately move back into the open space.

- The central players can quickly cut outside as soon as they sense the space is getting too tight.

Variations:

- Instead of a 1v1 (= cone), play 1v1 against a teammate.
- A *wall pass* with a teammate can precede the pass to the third player as an alternative to a dribble action.
- Increase the distances to provoke passes after the dribble actions.

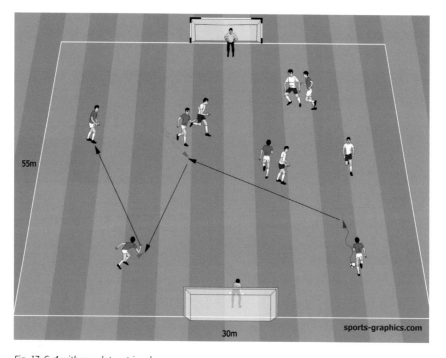

Fig. 17: 6v4 with mandatory triangle passes

Organization:

- 6v4 at two large goals with goalies on a playing field that is 55 x 30 m.
- Progression:
- The team with the superior number can only pass the ball on to a third player.
- The ball cannot be passed back to where it came from.
- The team with the inferior number is allowed to play together freely.

Coaching:

- The players must see the positioning on the field in width and depth.
- Also remember to look across the width of the field.

Variations:

- High degree of difficulty: The four players can only play *triangle passes*.
- The six players are limited to one or two touches.
- Return passes to the goalie are allowed.

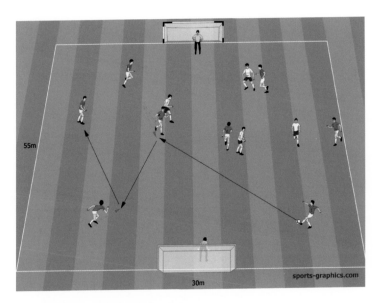

Fig. 18: 8v4 with one-touch and triangle passes

Organization:

- See fig. 17. The objective of this variation is for the player to let the ball do the work.

Progression:

- 8v4 where the eight players play with only one touch.
- The ball cannot be played back to the same player, resulting in play with opening actions.
- The team of four can play freely.

Coaching:

- Make sure the eight players' formation is orderly.
- Ask for *flat passes* because waist-high balls mean loss of time.
- The team with the superior numbers should prepare each scoring opportunity with precision.

Variations:

- Use time pressure: Every attack must be completed after 15 sec.
- Page 87
- The playing field is enlarged so more running effort is required (*passing fitness*).
- If a ball is played too high, the team with the inferior numbers gets to take a penalty kick.

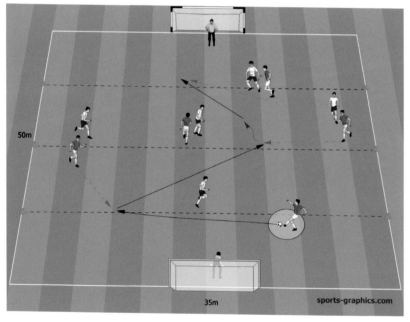

Fig. 19: 5v5: free and direct

Organization:

- 5v5 at two large goals with goalies on a field that is 50 x 35 m.
- The field is divided into four zones.

Progression:

- Both teams absolutely cannot pass back to the same player.
- Both teams always play free and direct. If the first player received the ball, the second player can only play it on with a direct pass.
- The ball also cannot be passed in one zone for too long. "Fast ball circulation!" (*Passing philosophy*)

Coaching:

- Demand positional discipline from the players (*passing tactics*).
- In a one-touch game pre-orientation (e.g., 360-degree view) by players is particularly important to the success of the game concept.
- Players should not demand only passes to the foot.

Variations:

- The players who must play with one touch are also allowed to pass back to the passing player.
- *The clock is running*: Every attack must end after 20 sec. During the switching phase, only 10 sec. remain until the shot at goal.
- *Open play* for all players, but the ball must be passed six times before a shot at goal can be taken.

Fig. 20: 6v6 plus 6

Organization:

- 6v6 plus 6 at two large goals with goalies on a playing field that is 60 x 40 m.

Progression:

- 6v6 with one and two touches.
- The 6v6 game is supplemented with six neutral players who position behind the goals (objective: provoking a long ball) and next to the field (objective: provoking the wide ball) (*passing tactics*).
- The neutral players play with the team in possession.
- The six neutral players get only one touch.
- The neutral players cannot pass to the player who passed the ball to them.

Coaching:

- Form *triangles* on the entire field.
- Focus on staggering individual parts of the team (*passing tactics*).
- The neutral player must also look across the width of the field.

Variations:

- Ask all players to play *flat passes.*

- The neutral players can also play among themselves. Objective: "Calm the game down!"

- *Open play* for the players on the field.

- The neutral players play with just one touch and must play the ball forward so a *third-man* scoring opportunity can be developed.

4.3.3 THE SWITCH PASS

> *"Technique is the spearhead of our basic training, and the foundation for everything else!"*
>
> (Michael Hordjik, athletic director at Underbouw and technical coach at Ajax Amsterdam; Münster, 2012).

In today's competitive game, the *switch pass* plays an important role in shifting plays. Because playing space in modern soccer continues to get smaller (tighter), the timed *switch pass* is a creative means for outplaying the opposing defense (*passing tactics*).

If you take the example of the 1-4-3-3-system with two real wingers, it is immediately obvious that in this system it makes sense to intersperse the *switch pass* so that the 7er and 11er can be used on the wing. Moreover today's competitive game requires the ability to get out of the grip of the opponent's defensive shifting to the ball with the help of the *switch pass*.

When finding and shifting in open spaces, the switch pass is one of the tools a well-trained soccer player has at his disposal. Furthermore, the appropriate and well-timed *wall* or *diagonal pass* is an effective option against an opponent who sits deep or with a changeover (*passing philosophy*).

The following fig. 21 shows a simulated switch pass situation, here played by Toni Kroos, as part of a changeover and shifting play from the inside left to the inside right in the 2012 DFB cup game between Borussia Mönchengladbach (here in white) and FC Bayern Munich (in red/white,) with a 0-0-score (action starts at 1:59 of playing time).

Fig. 21: Switch pass in the DFB championship game Borussia Mönchengladbach against FC Bayern Munich

EXAMPLES FOR PRACTICE AND INSTRUCTION

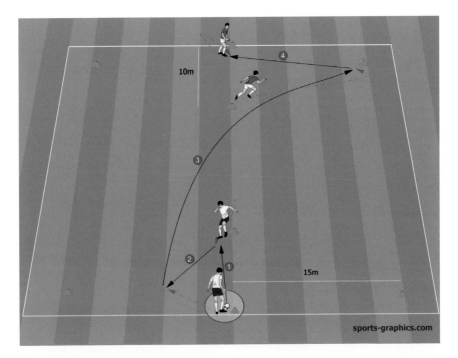

Fig. 22: Wide grid of four in switch pass mode

Organization:

- Four players.
- A total of eight cones; four of those are about 40 m apart.
- On two sides set up cones 2 x 2 centrally and approxmiately 10 m apart. The players position at the cones.
- Set up four cones to the sides of the centrally located 2-x-2 cones, approximately 15 m apart.

Progression:

- One player is positioned at each of the centrally located cones.
- The player in the circle has the ball and plays a short pass to the player across from him who lets the ball rebound diagonally into the running path.
- The player plays a *switch pass* to the left or right side (left or right cone) of the pair across from him.

- One of the pair runs after the *switch pass* and plays the ball back to his partner, who then plays a *switch pass* to the other side.
- A player chases down that ball to play it to another player, who then plays a *switch pass*.

Coaching:

- Rebounds from the short passes must be precise in order to properly prepare the *switch pass*.
- Incisive one-touch switch pass; play with both feet (*passing technique*).
- The *switch pass* should be played incisively, with speed and little spin.

Variations:

- The *switch pass* is played between the cones positioned at the center and the side.
- The *switch pass* is played with two touches, controlling and passing the ball.
- The *switch pass* should be accepted by a player who plays offensive 1v1 against his teammate and after winning the duel, plays the *switch pass* back.

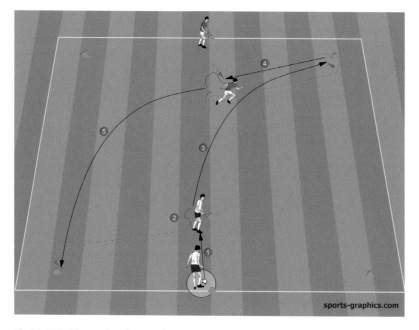

Fig. 23: Grid of four and cutting outside

Organization: See fig. 22.

Progression:
- See fig. 22. One player accepts the pass from his partner, immediately cuts outside, and plays the ball to the other side with a *switch pass.*
- The other player picks up the ball on the right or left side and lets it *bounce* off his partner, who then cuts outside.
- After each *switch pass* certain positional changes should be made between the individual pairs.

Coaching:
- Prepare your *switch pass* with a precise cutting (outside) action.
- *Use both feet to settle the ball* and *play a switch pass.*
- Keep up the pace while cutting outside and playing a *switch pass.*

Variations:
- The ball always stays in the air (perfecting technique).
- First cut outside, and then play offensive 1v1 against your partner followed by a *switch pass.*
- After turning away, one player plays a short pass to a teammate who then passes the ball deep to a teammate, who then plays the incisive and hard *switch pass* (*passing mindset*).

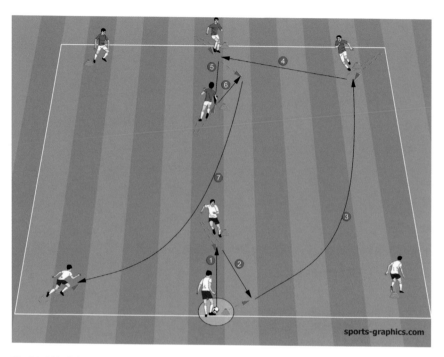

Fig. 24: Grid of eight with switch pass and rebounding elements

Organization:

- A total of eight cones and eight players (see fig. 22), and place the cones at increasing distances.

- A player is positioned at each cone.

- The player in the circle passes the ball to the partner facing him (see fig. 24) who lets the ball bounce diagonally into the running path of the passing player in the circle.

- He plays a *switch pass* to the outside left or right. The player positioned at these respective corners of the grid passes the ball across to the player diagonally opposite him, who plays a short pass (4) to the player opposite him.

- This player then lets the ball bounce back and then plays a *switch pass* to the outside left or right.

- Positional changes immediately take place within the respective group of four so that each player can play a *switch pass* and must resolve a *rebound situation* with a *passing technique*.

Coaching:

- Demand quick ball circulation.

- Also practice *switch passes* with the inside instep.

- Allow the blind *switch pass* (*passing mindset*).

Variations:

- Practice with two balls at the same time.

- The outside players at the side are replaced by goalies who can catch the ball and immediately pass it on.

- Allow *switch passes* on the ground (flat).

Cristiano Ronaldo playing a switch pass

Fig. 25: Grid of eight with switch pass variations

Organization: See fig. 24.

Progression:

- See fig. 24, particularly the player who receives the ball with a *switch pass* and then immediately passes it on to a teammate as a short pass.

Coaching:

- Players without the ball should always be at the ready.
- Players without the ball do not stand directly at the cone.
- Players who receive the *switch pass* immediately turn into the direction they want to play in.

Variations:

- The ball always stays in the air (very demanding on *passing technique*).
- Only play with one specific foot.
- Prior to the *switch pass* the group of four plays a quick Tiqui-Taca (see chapter 4.3.18), and only then play is shifted.

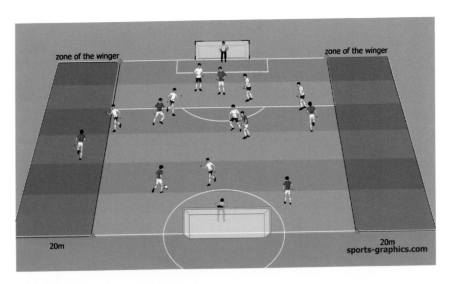

Fig. 26: 7v7 with mandatory switch passes

Organization:

- 7v7 play at two large goals on one half of a playing field.
- The two sides of the half field consist of 20-m-wide wing zones.

Progression:

- *Open play 7v7.*
- When a ball is played into the wing zone, it immediately must be played into the other wing zone with a *switch pass*.
- Only then can normal play resume.

Coaching:

- The on-ball foot immediately plays the *switch pass*.
- One of the players without the ball must immediately get open in the other wing zone so that he can accept the *switch pass*.
- Only play into the wing zones if the game situation permits it.

Variations:

- No attacking inside the wing zone.

- A goal counts if at least one *switch pass* was executed during play.

- Players are only allowed a total of one or two touches.

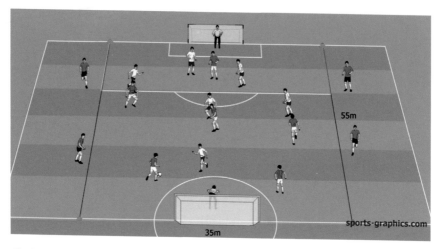

Fig. 27: 6v6 plus 4 wall-pass players

Organization:

- 6v6 at two large goals with goalies on a 55-x-35-m field.

Progression:

- 6v6 in a tactical formation to be determined.

- Four neutral players operate in the wing zones next to the playing field.

- The neutral players cooperate with the team in possession.

- As soon as a neutral player receives a pass, he must play a *switch pass* to the players in the other wing zone.

- The neutral players accept the ball and pass it back onto the playing field.

Coaching:

- Play a high-speed *switch pass* so a precise and quick shift in play can take place.

- Execute a situation-appropriate *switch pass* so the attacking team can reach the opposing goal more quickly.

- Intersperse the ball that is being passed into the wing zone as a *surprise ball* when playing space gets too tight (*passing tactics*).

Variations:

- After the *switch pass*, the receiver dribbles out of the wing zone onto the playing field, creating a 7v6 superior numbers game.
- After the *switch pass* into the other wing zone, an immediate cross in front of the opposing goal must be played from this zone to initiate a shot at goal.
- There are no neutral players in the wing zones. Instead one player from each team can operate there so that a *switch pass* must be won in a

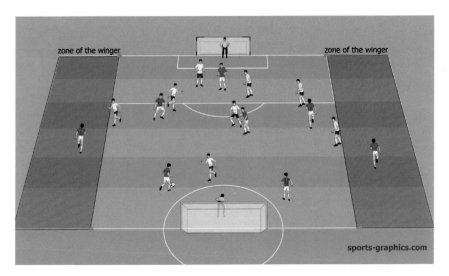

Fig. 28: 8v8 from switch pass to finish

Organization:

- 8v8 at two large goals with goalies on one half of a field.
- The field is divided into three vertical zones; two of these are marked as wing zones (see wing zone dimensions in fig. 28).

Progression:

- Open play 8v8.
- As soon as the ball is played into the wing zone, a *switch pass* follows.

- But this switch pass can also be played as an assist for a goal if the situation allows.

Coaching:

- The player must anticipate and decide if he wants to play the *switch pass* as an assist for a goal or as a means to shift play.
- If the *switch pass* is intended as an assist, it must be played very fast and with precision.
- If the *switch pass* is intended as a means to shift play, it cannot result in a hectic pace.

Variations:

- A goal can only be scored if the *switch pass* is played into the danger zone.
- After the *switch pass*, a neutral player is allowed onto the field, thereby creating a 9v8 superior numbers situation.
- *Switch passes* can only be played with the first touch.

4.3.4 THE VOLLEY PASS

"To me a pass is a kind of inner gratification!"

(Thomas Broich, former Bundesliga player with Mönchengladbach, Cologne, and Nuremberg, DFB-player, and current pro soccer player in Brisbane, Australia, from the movie *TOM MEETS ZIZOU - No Summer Fairytale.* Mindjazz Pictures, 2011)

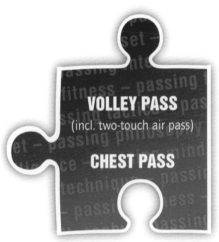

Any ball that is played directly out of the air requires the utmost precision, body tension, visual perception, and anticipation and balance. In soccer practice,this type of passing from the air using the foot (see chapter 4.3.4.2), the head (see chapter 4.3.14), or the chest (see chapter 4.3.4.1) is referred to as a *volley.*

Due to the current developments and future prospects in national and international soccer (men, youth, Futsal), the volley is gaining more attention in soccer instruction and advanced training (see chapter 2; FIFA 2010 and 2011; UEFA 2012a and b; Süddeutsche.de 2013). Approximately 37% of all goals in the 2011/2012 Champions League season came from crosses and *long balls* (UEFA 2012, pg. 10), particularly because crosses and *long balls* (especially for defense) are becoming much more prominent in modern and future attacking play. *Volley passes* are

- shot at goal with the foot (e.g., after a high cross),
- passed with control after an *up-and-over pass* to a teammate,
- used as the next to last pass (see Knievel 2011),
- used to clear after a *chip pass* behind the defense, and
- settle the ball, for instance with the chest, to play it on with a *flat pass.*

As can be seen from these examples, the *volley* in all its facets is very demanding in terms of *passing techniques*, spatial and temporal pressure (with increased pressing near the goal by the opponent), and the players' mindset with increasing stress (e.g., in the *danger zone*).

Here we focus on the volley pass that is played either as a *chest pass* (see chapter 4.3.4.1) or as a *lofted pass* (see chapter 4.3.4.2) in soccer. For clarity and specificity, the header will be described in detail as a separate puzzle in chapter 4.3.14.

Team Germany player Thomas Müller playing a volley pass during practice

4.3.4.1   THE CHEST PASS

Dortmund player Ilkay Gündogan playing a chest pass

This type of pass allows the player to forward the ball with his chest. Forwarding the ball is usually combined with settling and controlling the ball ("Settle it and bring it down to the ground.").

A pass to the 9er in the attacking center is a typical game situation. In this situation the 9er likes to let the ball rebound from his chest to the approaching 10er to develop a direct shot at goal (e.g., shot at goal from the second line, give-and-go, give-and-follow, pass behind the back line) (*passing tactics and philosophy*).

In youth training the coach or instructor should teach the chest pass to be intuitive because many players at the beginning of their soccer training develop a kind of fear of the ball coming toward them at head or chest level. This is because of the body's natural protective mechanisms and therefore must be taken into account in soccer training (*passing mindset*).

The following fig. 29 shows a simulated *chest pass* situation at a full sprint into the running path by the FC Arsenal London's fullback in response to a switch pass from right to left, in the Champions League game between Arsenal London (here in red/white) against FC Barcelona (here in white/blue) from Feb. 2, 2011, with a score of 0-1 (start of action at 77:36 minutes of playing time).

Fig. 29: Switch pass (chapter 4.3.3) and chest pass (chapter 4.3.4.1) from the Champions League game Arsenal London against FC Barcelona

EXAMPLES FOR PRACTICE AND INSTRUCTION

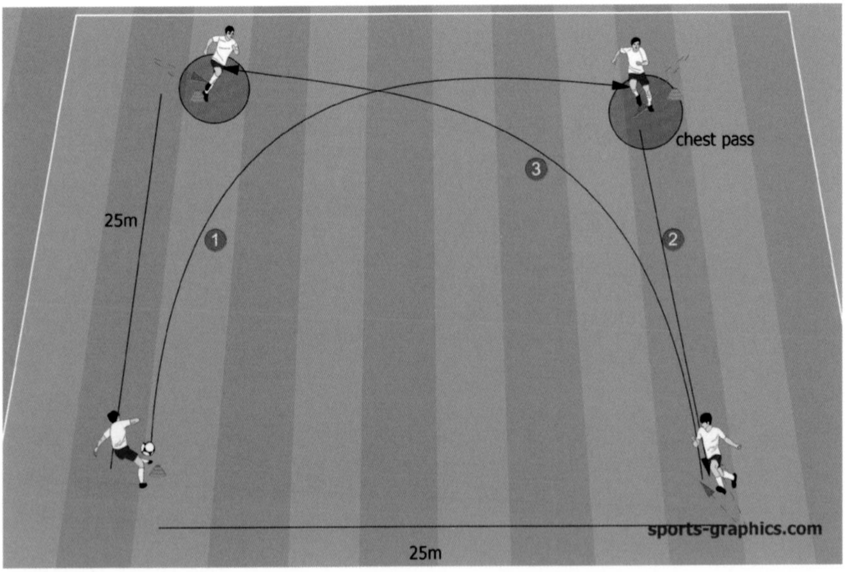

Fig. 30: Grid of four and chest pass

Organization:

- Set up four cones approximately 25 m apart.
- A player is positioned at each cone (four players total).

Progression:

- The player in the circle passes the ball to the player standing diagonally across from him, who then lets the ball rebound to the teammate with a *chest pass*. He comes toward the ball, settles it into the new passing direction, and passes the ball to another teammate.

Coaching:

- The player without the ball should make some space for himself.
- Precision in passing the ball on with the chest so that the subsequent *switch pass* can be played directly.
- Play additional *switch passes* so that timing and exertion for the *chest pass* are easier to control (*passing technique*).

Variations:

- Own assist with the chest and then playing the ball back (see simulated situation).
- Own assist with the chest and passing to a teammate who then lobs the ball so that it can be passed with the chest, and only then is the *switch pass* played.
- Competition: Set up two grids side by side. Determine which players play the fastest grid of four (measure the time).

Fig. 31: 5v5 plus 4 chest pass players

Organization:

- 5v5 at two large goals with goalies on a playing field that is 40 x 30 m.

Progression:

- Open play 5v5.
- A player stands on either side of each goal. They are extra forwards.
- After receiving the pass, the extra forwards must pass the ball on with a *chest pass.*

Coaching:

- The *chest pass* players must create space situationally so they are able to play an incisive and well-timed *chest pass*.
- The *chest pass* player must spot the third player before the ball is passed to him.
- "Focus on body tension!'

Variations:

- The neutral player can also settle the ball with the chest and then pass it on: "Ball control is the top priority!"
- The neutral player settles the pass with the chest, plays the ball into his own running path, and then plays on the field as the superior number player.
- The neutral player does his own assist and immediately tries to score.
- The neutral players are positioned at the sides of the field, receive a *switch pass,* and after doing their own *chest pass* move onto the field with a fast dribble, creating superior numbers and pressure from the outside (passing technique).
- Pairing up: Let the *chest pass* rebound to the back and create double the superior numbers.
- The goalie opens the game with a pass to the 9er (in a formation with a striker) who lets the ball *rebound* with his chest to the approaching 10er, who can then initiate a shot at goal while facing the opposing goal.
- Opening the game via the central defenders or fullbacks, same progression as previous variation.

4.3.4.2 THE LOFTED PASS

EXAMPLES FOR PRACTICE AND INSTRUCTION

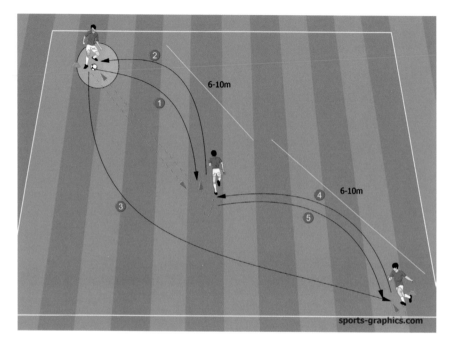

Fig. 32: Grid of three with volley passes

Organization:

Three players stand facing each other on a diagonal (or straight line) approximately 6-10 m apart.

Progression:

- The player in the circle first lofts the ball for himself and then passes it to his teammate with a *volley pass*; that player lets the pass *rebound*.
- The player in the circle now plays a high *volley pass* to the third teammate.
- In the meantime both players switch positions.

Coaching:

- *"Only play volley passes!"* (passing technique)
- Variations in *passing technique* (inside-foot kick, inside-instep and laces kick)
- Get into ready position.
- Play *push passes* (fast passes in passing direction).

Variations:

- Use two mandatory touches.
- Play volley passes only with the left or the right foot.
- Change distances from each other.

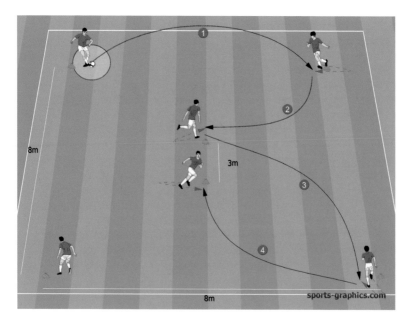

Fig. 33: Grid of six with volley passes

Organization:

- Form a grid of six in which six players practice.
- Distance between outside cones is approximately 8 m; between inside cones is approxmiately 3 m.

Progression:

- The player in the circle plays the ball (see fig. 32) to the player to his left, who sets up to a player in the center with a short *volley pass*.
- The center player can choose between a *volley pass* to the player in the circle or a *volley pass* into the other triangle.

Coaching:

- "Never wait at the cone!" (*passing fitness*)
- "Not too much spin or rotation on the volley pass!" (*passing technique*)
- Practice with both feet (*passing technique*).

Variations:

- Practice with two balls.

- Permanent position changes (*passing fitness*).

- Integrate flat passes (*passing technique*).

Fig. 34: Volley passes and shots at goal

Organization:

Five players (plus one supplemental player) practice on one large goal with goalie.

Progression:

- The player in the circle passes the ball to the player on the wing who bounces the ball back.

- The player plays a *precise cross* to the third player in the direction of the back post.

- This player plays a *volley pass* to the player in the penalty box or in the back who finishes.

Coaching:

- "Play all passes very fast!"
- "Carefully targeted volley passes."
- "Player without the ball: quick footwork!"

Variations:

- 1v1 in the center.
- The player at the back post has the opportunity to score the goal with a *volley shot.*
- Add another large goal with goalie. Attackers *actively switch play* with a turnover and prevent the defenders from playing at the (additional) large goal.

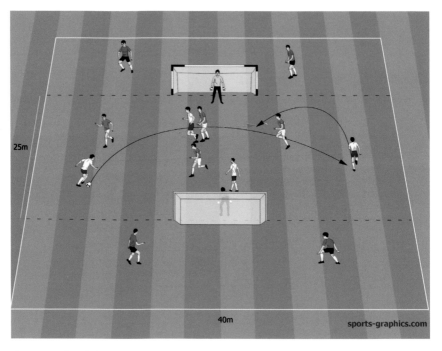

Fig. 35: 4v4 plus 4 lofted pass

Organization:

- 4v4 at two large goals with goalies on a playing field that is 40 x 25 m.
- Four neutral players are positioned behind the two goals.

Progression:

- On the field the ball can only be played high.
- Shots are taken by *volley* (from the air) and only with the feet.
- The neutral players should
    a. also receive the ball only from the air and keep it up and
    b. only bring the ball to the ground when they want to calm down" the game.

In case of b), a *switch pass* is played to the goalie on the opposite side and the game continues.

Coaching:

- "Create spaces!" (*Passing tactics*)
- "Don't be afraid of risky passes!" (*Passing mindset*)
- "Execute pre and post-actions!" (*Passing fitness*)

Variations:

- Open play follows whenever the neutral players take the volley pass low to the ground, meaning the ball cannot bounce on the ground.
- 5v3 in which the five players can only play *lofted passes* and the three players can only play *flat passes* (*passing technique*).
- If a neutral player plays the ball back onto the field, it is immediately followed by a shot at goal.

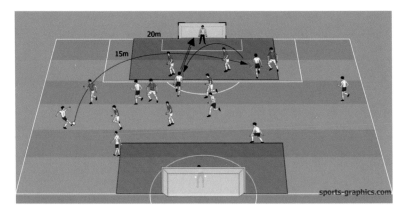

Fig. 36: 8v8 with a deep volley pass zone

Organization:

- 8v8 at two large goals with goalies on one half of a field.
- There is a 20-x-15-m deep *volley pass zone* in front of each goal.

Progression:

- Open play.
- A goal can be scored only when the ball is played high into the *volley pass zone*.
- The team in possession must pass the ball high (and without touching the ground) at least once in the volley pass zone.
- After that a shot at goal can be taken.

Coaching:

- "No blind passes into the *volley pass zone*, but rather prepare the pass into the volley pass zone!" (*Passing tactics*)
- "Pay close attention to plays to the *back post*!"
- "The 9er must try to quickly *go to the ball from the back*!" (*Passing philosophy*)

Variations:

- Shots at goal can be taken from the second line (element of surprise, originality).
- Direct kick in the volley pass zone! (*Passing mindset*)
- A point is scored when the ball is passed inside the *volley pass zone* (*second to last pass, passing mindset*)

Fig. 37: 11v11 with assist, next to last action, and goal scored with the help of a volley pass

Organization:

- 11v11 on a three-quarter field with two large goals and two goalies.

Progression:

- Open play.
- A goal can only be scored when the next to last action and the final action, the goal, are played out of the air.

Coaching:

- Use *chip balls* and *switch passes* as preparation (*assists*) (*passing technique*).
- Lofted-pass players: "Pay attention to body tension and situational arm and leg use in terms of maintaining balance!" (*Passing fitness*)
- "Head up, look around: where is the third man?" (*Passing intelligence*)

Variations:

- Decrease the field size so that the players are able to develop more goal box scenarios: "The closer to the goal the action, the more creative it is" (Memmert, 2013d, pg. 103).

- Contrast: On the field the ball is kept high, but to get off a shot, in this case the finish, a flat pass must also be played (*high degree of difficulty*).
- Headers are allowed (*creativity*).

4.3.5 THE NO-LOOK PASS

"Liverpool FC could be summed up in just three words: Pass and move!"

(Alan Hansen, 2007, n.t. and s.l.)

In competitive play, the *no-look pass* is a type of diversionary tactic for the opponent. The ball is passed in the direction where the player is not looking. This requires the players to be able to distribute and pass the ball unimpeded and with a variable *passing technique*. Conversely the opposing players must learn to train their ability to split their attention when a player makes a *no-look pass* (*passing intelligence and tactics*).

Players enjoy trying out techniques and behavior patterns that are new and different during practice or training. This includes disguising one's true intention—deceit using the *no-look pass* within the rules of the game. Practice and training should provide players with space and opportunity to develop nuanced perceptual and technical decision-making processes because these also tap into resources that can be advantageous to an interesting and successful game (*passing technique and mindset*).

The following fig. 38 shows the simulated *no-look pass* situation of the Brazilian 9er in the center of the opponent's attacking half (here Brazil in white/blue) against the Netherlands (here in red/white) from July 2, 2010, at the FIFA World Cup with a score of 0-0 (start of action at 7:07 minutes of playing time).

Fig. 38: The no-look pass in the 2010 FIFA World Cup game between Brazil and the Netherlands

The Brazilian player made the *no-look pass* into the seam (between the two Dutch central defenders). The left winger sprinting into the space was then able to successfully use the open space behind the defensive line for a fast dribble with a subsequent 1v1 against the goalie, followed by an *assist pass* to one of the two teammates moving up (see chapter 4.3.7).

The *no-look pass* made it possible for the Brazilian three-man attacking line to successfully score within 5 seconds against the Netherlands' five defenders.

EXAMPLES FOR PRACTICE AND INSTRUCTION

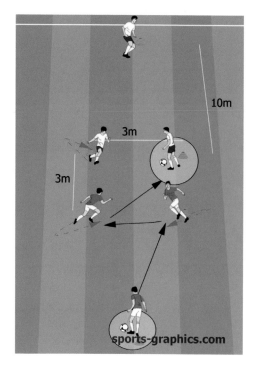

Fig. 39: The grid of six with no-look passes

Organization:

- Four cones are set up in a square approximately 3 m apart.
- Two more cones are set up about 10 m from the square, forming two mirror triangles apprxomiately 3 m apart.
- A player is positioned at each of the six cones.

Progression:

- All six players play simultaneously.
- Players play with two balls that initially circulate between the groups of three (in the two triangles).
- In addition, the two balls should be continuously switched back and forth between the two groups of three, creating passing confusion.
- Players should play *no-look passes* to each other with the two balls to purposely surprise the player without the ball.

Coaching:

■ Practice the *no-look pass* with speed and focus, not putting on a show.

■ Play the ball incisively and low to the ground.

■ Immediately be ready again after the pass because there are two balls in play.

Variations:

■ Practice with one ball.

■ Only play the *no-look pass* to open up the drill. Motto: "Create a surprise!" (*Passing philosophy*)

■ Play *no-look passes* and combine and execute them with a position change: "Run to where you did not pass the ball!"

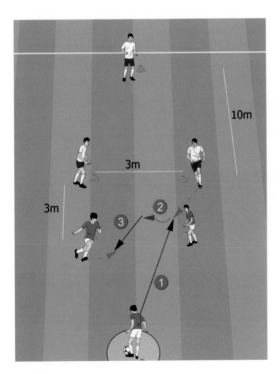

Fig. 40: Grid of six with dribbling and no-look pass

Organization: See fig. 39.

Progression:

■ Do the drill with one ball.

- Players without the ball stand *behind* or *between* the cones. By doing so they create more space and are able to dribble again immediately after the *no-look pass* and then use the *no-look pass*.

Coaching:

- "Already think about where you want to play the ball while you are dribbling!"
- "Don't dribble to where you intend to pass the ball!"
- "Emotional control (calm) on the ball!"

Variations:

- Execute a *no-look feint* first and then pass.
- After the dribble the coach tells the player where to pass the ball (adding the *auditory analyzer*).
- Practice with two balls.

Fig. 41: 8v8 with four no-look goals

Organization:

- 8v8 at four large goals on one half of a field with a goalie in each.

Progression:

- The team in red/white as well as the one in white/blue play at two goals, or rather defend two goals.

- Every ball played as a *no-look pass* that reaches the teammate is rewarded with one point.
- Five points are awarded if a *no-look pass* results in a goal.

Coaching:

- "Only play the *no-look pass* when the game situation allows it."
- "If the space is very tight, consider a *no-look pass*."
- "Make sure that the *no-look pass* does not significantly increase the rate of passing errors." (*Passing philosophy*)

Variations:

- Both teams can play at all goals and score there.
- The coach, the team leader, or the goalies announce which team can or must play at which goal (*adding the auditory analyzers*).
- If a player scores with a *no-look shot*, his team is awarded 10 points.

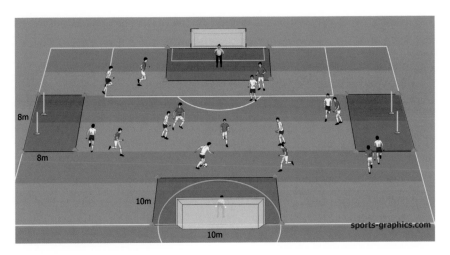

Fig. 42: 8v8 with no-look dribble goals

Organization:

- 8v8 at two large goals with goalies and two pole goals without goalies on one half of a field.

119

- Each of the two large goals gets a 10-x-10-m-wide zone marked with cones. Semi circles can be marked as an alternative.
- The two pole goals get an 8-x-8-m-wide zone.

Progression:

- One team defends the pole goals and the other team defends the two large goals.
- Open play.
- When a *no-look pass* is played into one of the four zones, the player receiving the ball in that zone cannot be attacked by an opposing outfield player.
- A 1v1 against the goalie must then follow in the zone in front of the large goal.

Coaching:

- Use the *no-look pass* as a preparatory element for the finish (*passing philosophy*).
- Use the *no-look pass* if you want to prevent your team from stereotypical attacking play and surprise (and unsettle) the opponent. (*passing philosophy*).
- Play the *no-look pass* fearlessly (*passing mindset*).
- "Don't be afraid of *no-look passes* that initially miss their target!" (*passing mindset*)

Variations:

- Play with one or two touches.
- Play with one or two touches and also with an assist so that after two touches the game can only be continued with a *no-look pass*.
- Five extra points are awarded if the goalie is beaten with a *no-look shot*.

4.3.6 THE FLAT AND COMBINATION PASS (SHORT PASS)

"If God wanted us to play soccer in heaven he would have grown grass there!"

(Brian Clough on playing high balls; deceased legendary English player and coach, FC Sunderland, FC Middlesbrough, Derby County, Leeds United).

Why do so many spectators come to the games, and why do so many sports writers write and report so enthusiastically at so many soccer games? No doubt because of the great goals! But how to prepare for those? With lots of confident and incisive combinations (*combination passes*), *creative assists*, the next-to-last pass (see Memmert, 2013d, pg. 103), and *playing with the third man* (*passing philosophy*). Moreover, since the 2010 World Cup in South Africa we know that the pass into the seams, played as a *flat pass*,

"[...] has become instrumental in generating goal threats" (see Memmert, 2013d, pg. 103; Knievel 2011).

And what does a game look like when a player wants to keep possession because he doesn't feel like leaving the initiative to the opponent or just wants to be boss on the ball or just quickly reenergize his own team? It has countless *flat passes* that, paired with the sure ball control and settling, ensure and display the desired flow (*passing mindset* and *tactics*).

And what does the C-league youth player wish for when he stands in front of the opposing goal? A level ground pass (*flat pass*) so he can easily and safely push the ball with precision into the goal. After all, the ball is supposed to regularly find the back of the net, and what youth trainer wants to frequently see a waist-high to high, poorly-timed and sudden pass at the start of a soccer career cause tears of disappointment in a player in front of the opposing goal and gloating by the opposing team (along with the coach and spectators).

We want to help create a sense of achievement by subsequently bringing in numerous examples for practice and instruction that are meant to motivate regular use of *flat and combination passes*. This also includes the element of *ball control*, which, particularly in passing play, is a hinge function whose purpose is the efficient continuation of play (e.g., again with a pass).

With respect to *ball control* in *flat and combination passes*, getting in the open and closed position plays a central role. The pass sequence with five or the grid of 20 are viable options in line with the aspect of repetition of the previously mentioned fundamentals within large practice groups and classes. For the interested reader this information is shown and illustrated below in tables and in compressed form for training purposes (table 1).

Table 1: Ball control technique and tactics

CLOSED POSITION 1	CLOSED POSITION 2	CLOSED POSITION 3
Turning: The opponent is too close to the player.	Secure and carry the ball: Opponent without error.	Carry the ball to shift play.
Putting your back into the opponent to block him from the ball; turning around him while controlling the ball.	Move diagonally backward to get into a lateral position from which a dribbling, shooting, or passing option arises.	Carry the ball against the defenders' movements on the inside line to the open side. All options taken from a lateral position.

OPEN POSITION 1	OPEN POSITION 2	OPEN POSITION 3
Carry the ball past the opponent.	Carrying the ball into the opponent's path.	Carrying the ball in a dribble toward the opponent.
The opponent approaches too quickly. The attacker speeds up as soon as he touches the ball and moves past the opponent.	The opponent approaches too quickly from the side to confront the attacker.	The opponent allows space; the attacker dribbles toward him to tie him up before the pass.
	The attacker moves the ball past him.	

The following fig. 43 shows the simulated situation of a *third man pass* executed after a *throw-in pass* by a player from Arsenal London (see chapter 4.3.15) using *flat and combination passes* in the Champions League game Arsenal London against BV Borussia Dortmund, Nov. 23, 2011, at a 0-0 score in a tight space on the right wing (action starts at 8:57 minutes of playing time).

Fig. 43: Flat and combination passes after a throw-in pass in the Champions League game Arsenal London vs. BV Borussia Dortmund 09

EXAMPLES FOR PRACTICE AND INSTRUCTION

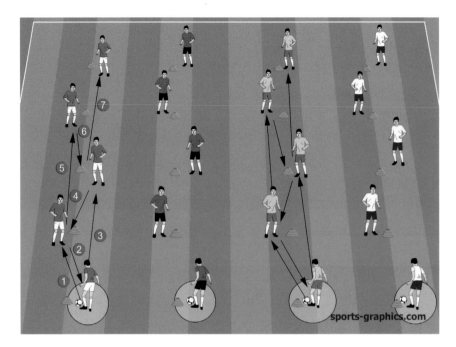

Fig. 44: Grid of 20 with lots of flat and combination passes from a closed position

Organization:

- 20 cones are set up in five rows with four cones in each row.
- The distance between the five and four cones respective to each other, vertically and horizontally, is approximately 5 m. A player is positioned at each cone (20 players total).

Progression:

- Five players in one row are given a colored bib, so four teams with four different colors can be seen on the field.
- The five players in each row practice together.
- Player 1 in the circle passes the ball to the teammate who lets the ball *rebound*, and the player in the circle passes the ball to the player after the next player (skipping a row), and so on.

Coaching:

- The players should not stay directly next to the cone but move sideways to create a passing angle (a diagonal).
- In addition, the pass should not be played to the body but rather next to the playing leg of the receiving player.
- Pre-actions are mandatory (see chapter 4.5).

Variations:

- Play with two touches.
- Play with two touches and both feet.
- The first touch should stop the ball dead (ball should be still) and then be played with the sole of the foot (in the style of Futsal).

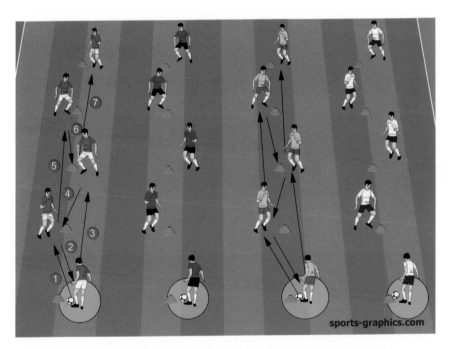

Fig. 45: Grid of 20 with lots of flat and combination passes from an open and half-open position

Organization: See fig. 44.

Progression:

See fig. 44 in which the players without a ball wait for the ball in the *open position* and after receiving it, play it on.

Coaching:

- Players should not stand directly next to the cone but rather move sideways.
- Add modifications: Alternate the *on-ball* and *off-ball* playing leg.
- Minimize ball rotation; passing speed and precision are desired (*passing technique*).

Variations:

- One-touch passing.
- Two-touch passing.
- Settle the ball, do a scissor (feint), and then pass it on.

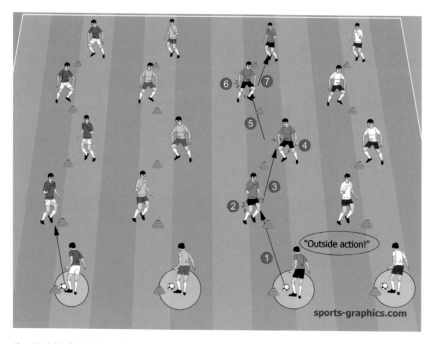

Fig. 46: Grid of 20 with cutting outside actions

Organization: See fig. 44.

Progression:

See fig. 44 in which the players should not let the ball *rebound*. Instead they immediately cut outside after the pass to be able to play the next *short pass* to a teammate.

Coaching:

- "Quick cut outside and slow *short pass*!"
- Ask for some slow and some quick *short passes*.
- The player without the ball should make some space.

Variations:

- Turn the ball with the sole of the foot and play the pass with the inside foot.
- Turn the ball with the inside foot and play the pass with the outside foot (*Brazilian passing*).
- Cut outside, sidestep the cone, and then play the first pass. Motto: Cut, feint, and pass in a tight space!

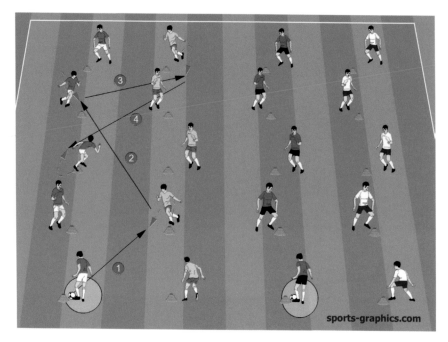

Fig. 47: Grid of 20 with crossover passing

Organization: See fig. 44.

Progression:

- Expanded side-by-side team play: Team 1 with team 2, and team 3 with team 4 (*10-man passing game*).
- No guidelines. Players look for passing solutions. The coach or instructor does not provide solutions. The players must actively create passing solutions (see chapter 4.5).

Coaching:

- Vary the ball speed.
- Pre-action: "Standing by the cone is a *No-Go!*"
- Post-action: "360-degree orientation and always be ready for the next pass."

Variations:

- Practice in the *closed position*.
- Practice in the *open position*.

- Passing confusion: Here, for instance, player 1 can also pass to player 3 of the other team.

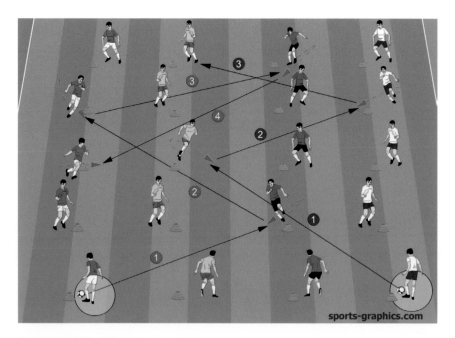

Fig. 48: Grid of 20 with longer crossover passes

Organization: See fig. 47.

Progression:

- Team 1 plays with team 3, and team 2 plays with team 4.
- The players stay in their positions next to the cones, but they continue to execute *pre- and post-actions* (*passing fitness and tactics*).
- The players without the ball must get out of the way as there are always two balls circulating.

Coaching:

- Players should be primarily in the *open position* so they can be aware of both balls.
- Vary the passing speed.
- Active and audible coaching among players to convey readiness for active support.

Variations:

- The players pass the balls and afterward move to a new position.

- Specify different touch limits.

- Execute fast sprints after the pass between two cones to initiate *passing fitness*.

Fig. 49: 5v5 plus 10—only flat passes are allowed.

Organization:

- See fig. 47.

- The center cones are taken out of the grid of 20 to form a tighter playing field.

Progression:

- Team 1 plays for possession against team 2.

- Team 3 and team 4 stand next to the playing field near the cones as neutral players and play with only one touch with the team in possession.

Coaching:

- Flat passes are mandatory for all players.

- Players without the ball should always get out of the *cover shadow*.
- After a pass the respective player immediately begins a *post-action* and actively calls for the ball.
- Form lots of triangles.

Variations:

- Reverse the rules of play. Intention: Neutral players on the outside calm down the game with unrestricted touches.
- In 5v5, the ball cannot be played back to the same teammate (use *triangle passes*).
- Teams immediately switch if the ball is played high.

Fig. 50: 10v5 plus 5 (playing with superior numbers and flat passes)

Organization:

- See fig. 49.
- The size of the field increases slightly.

Progression:

- Team 1 and team 2 play together against team 3.

- Team 4 is outside the playing field.
- Team 1 and team 2 are not allowed to pass to the neutral players (team 4). They only pass to each other using *flat passes*.
- The superior numbers team plays with only one touch.
- When the outnumbered team wins possession, they play together with the neutral players.
- The coach can specify a playing period or make a rule that with a turnover, team 1 or 2 must immediately switch with the neutral players.

Coaching:

- Position play.
- Superior numbers must let the ball do the work.
- Immediately start *counter pressing* after a turnover.

Variations:

- Superior numbers team must continuously choose new players among themselves to pass the ball.
- Superior numbers team plays with two mandatory touches.
- Whenever the outnumbered team is able to keep the ball within their own ranks 5 times, they score a bonus point. The same is retained: Which outnumbered team (role change) scores the most bonus points?

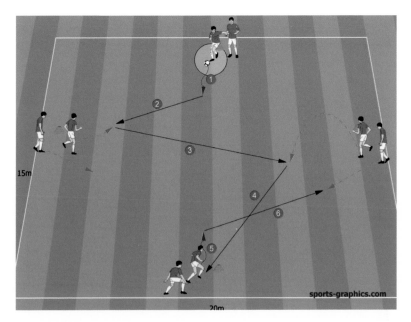

Fig. 51: Grid of four with continuous passing

Organization:

- A 20 x 15 m diamond.
- Four players plus substitutes are positioned at the cones.

Progression:

- The player in the circle is in possession and starts to dribble.
- The two players next to him execute *pre-actions opposite* the direction of the player in possession and offer support in an *open position*.
- The payer in possession plays a *flat pass* to the player on his right who then plays a diagonal *flat pass* to the third player who is turning around and then passes to the fourth player in the diamond.

Coaching:

- Players without the ball must offer their support in a *precise, open position*.
- *Flat passes* with little spin (*passing technique*).
- "Mandatory passing with both feet!"

Variations:

- Continuous passing with two touches per player.
- Position two players in the diamond approximately 10 m apart so that the *flat pass* has to be played farther and with more *force (varied exertion)*.
- The third player in the diamond plays the ball back to the player in the circle so that the ball is played to the fourth player afterward with an opening pass *(varied conditions)*.

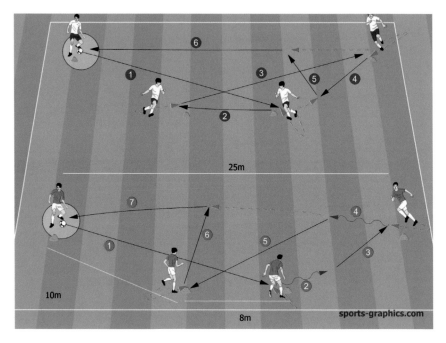

Fig. 52: Grid of four in back-four formation with rebound or cut during continuous passing

Organization:

- Set up cones 2 x 4 at a distance of approximately 8 m (cones inside-inside), approximately 10 m (cones inside-outside), and approximately 25 m (cones outside-outside), and man each with one player.
- If more than 2 x 4 players are actively participating, they move to the respective starting positions (see colored circles).

Progression:

- See fig. 51 with specified sequence (1, 2 ...), in which the first *flat pass* is carried into a dribble by cutting (see back-four formation) or the player lets it *rebound* to the inside. The player that is initially skipped (bottom left) verbally coaches this decision: "Rebound!" or "Cut!" If the ball is passed to the right outside, the *flat-pass player* again coaches the receiving player with "Rebound!" or "Cut!" so that a *double-pass* can be played.
- If the starting position is at least double-manned, the players run after their respective *flat passes* (*permanent position change*).

Variation:

- Change the starting position.
- Change the distances between cones.
- Change the geometry.
- Replace the codes "Rebound!" and "Cut!" with other synonyms (unfamiliar to the opponent).
- The final pass takes place as a follow-up action into a small or large goal (with and without goalie), or against a bench or over one goal into another small goal, or the like.

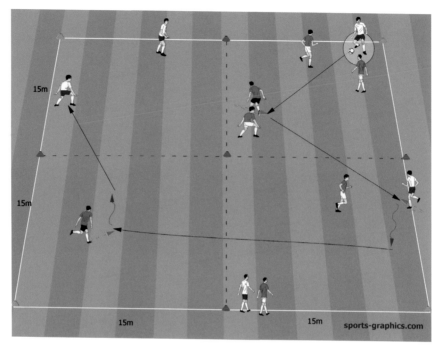

Fig. 53: Looking for flat passes to a third player

Organization:

5v5 with two neutral players on a playing field that is 30 x 30 m and divided into four squares of equal size.

Progression:

- *Open flat-pass play* in which the ball can be in one quarter for no more than 5 sec.
- The neutral players play with only one touch.
- If a team with the two neutral players is able to make three direct passes to a third player, it scores one point.
- Determine which team is able to score the most points in, for instance, 4 min.

Variations:

- If one team scores three points in a row, meaning the opposing team does not get possession, it is awarded a goal.
- Use goalies as neutral players (the goalie as sweeper).

- Set up four small goals 8-10 m apart (from the square's touchline) in all directions, and when
    - a) a point is scored, or
    - b) a goal is scored (3 points in a row)

  players are allowed to play out of the square directly at one of the small goals with a fast and incisive *flat pass*. If the team scores they are awarded another point.
- Set up the same way but with increased distance to the small goals in which the fast and incisive *flat pass* must be played into a teammate's running path (keep in mind the offside rule), who must then put the passed ball directly into a small goal without difficulty (but with speed). If he scores the team is awarded two more points.
- Set up the same way but include large goals with goalie and open finish.

Munich's Bastian Schweinsteiger plays a flat pass.

Fig. 54: Four-zone passing

Organization:

- 9v9 at two large goals with goalie on a three-quarter field.
- The playing field is divided into *four lateral zones.*

Progression:

- Both teams play only *flat passes.*
- The ball can only be passed from zone to zone.
- Goals can only be scored from the last (offensive) zone.

Coaching:

- Ask for lots of cutting actions in the various zones.
- Get into the *open position* as much as is situationally possible to generate lots of one-touch actions.
- Teammates should frequently play *flat passes* next to the player's body so he can cut quickly and with precision.

Variations:

- The ball must be passed three times in a row in one zone before switching to another zone.
- The ball cannot be passed back.
- As soon as the ball is passed high, the opponent gets a penalty kick.

Fig. 55: Four-zone passing (dribble or open pass)

Organization: See fig. 54.

Progression:

- The ball can now be played across two zones with a *flat pass*.
- The ball can now also be dribbled into the next zone.

Coaching:

- Make *quick* decisions.
- *Dribbling* must be done at high speed.
- Play *flat passes* into seams (also in the center) between opposing players.

Variations:

- Coach or players impose different *touch limits* (aspects of personal responsibility and independence).

- Shot at opposing goal can only be taken after 45 sec; practice composure and domination via possession (*passing mindset*).

- During an offensive changeover phase, the shot at the opposing goal must be taken after 10 sec. (develop train track-mindset).

Fig. 56: Four-zone passing (holding on to the ball and using open ground passes)[1]

Organization: See fig. 54.

Progression:

- The ball can be played as a *ground pass* in all directions.

- Rule: First pass the ball to each other three times in a row in one zone, and after that the ball can be passed out of the zone with a *ground pass.*

---

13 *The term ground pass is the synonym for the flat pass. It illustrates the simple and precise pass, particularly for youth players (point of impact playing soccer in the center and most often with the broad side).*

Coaching:

- Ask for eager and coordinated pre- and post-actions in one zone.
- "Get out of the opponent's cover shadow often!"
- "Don't hold on to the ball too long!"

Variations:

- Play with only one to two touches.
- Zones can be expanded if the game doesn't *flow*.
- The ball can no longer be played into a back zone.

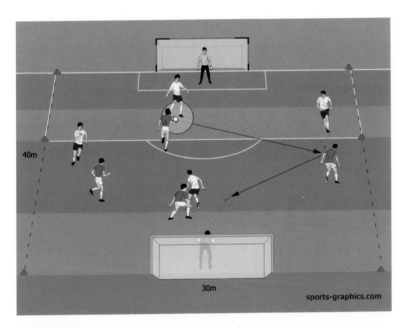

Fig. 57: 4v4 tournament: Only ground passes are allowed!

Organization:

- 4v4 at two large goals with goalie on a playing field that is 40 x 30 m.

Progression:

- 4v4 is played out in a tournament format with four teams (2 x A-B, C-D, 2 x A-C, B-D, and 2 x A-D and B-C).
- 2 min. of playing time per game.

Coaching:

- "Use only *ground passes*!"
- "Look for playing solutions!"
- The (playing) goalie must always *open* the game again.
- "If no gap to the front opens up, stay calm on the ball and look for other solutions!"

Variations:

- The coach or the players together determine playing times and touch limits.
- "No back-passes to the goalie!
- "The finish must come from one touch!"

Fig. 58: 4v4 tournament: Use ground passes exclusively!

Organization:

- 4v4 at two large goals with goalie on a playing field that is 40 x 25 m.

Progression:

- 4v4 in which four additional players stand next to the playing field and play together with the team of four in possession with just one touch.
- The neutral players can also only play *ground passes.*

Coaching:

- The neutral players also must anticipate the *third man.*
- The neutral players must always *reopen* the game.
- The players on the field should not group so much in tight spaces but rather take advantage of and maximize superior number situations.

Variations:

- The neutral players can also play high balls.
- The neutral players cannot play the ball back to the same player.
- When a neutral player gets possession, he can move onto the field and play with the superior numbers until the finish.

11V11 ON ONE HALF OF A LARGE FIELD: USE GROUND PASSES ONLY!

Organization:

- 11v11 at two large goals with goalies on one half of a large playing field.

Progression:

- The ball can only be passed with a *ground pass.*
- If a *ground pass* does not make it to a teammate, the following rules go into effect:
    1. *Corner kick*
    2. *Free kick*
    3. *Penalty kick for the opponent*

Coaching:

- The small playing area requires corresponding strategic positional play.
- "Form lots of *triangles*!"
- "Pay attention to *pre- and post-actions*!"

Variations:

- The finish is disconnected from the *flat-pass play*; high balls on the goal are allowed.
- The ball can only be passed in *playing direction*.
- 9v9 plus two neutral players in which the superior numbers team only plays with one to two touches and *ground passes*.

4.3.6.1 FLAT PASS SPECIAL

A more differentiated analysis and description of modern passing training are advisable when considering *flat-pass play* and not just *short-* and *combination-pass play*. This is provided in the form of a *special*.

The effective *advantages* of *flat-pass* play are obvious:

- It facilitates quick *passing combinations* and the sure and precise path to the finish (e.g., in the danger zone).
- Flat passes played into the running path open up dynamic fast pace actions.
- It is easier to keep the ball in the possession team's ranks (securing results, varying pace).
- As a result the opponent must give chase (attrition tactic, provoke errors).
- High and waist-high passes are very demanding for the receiver in terms of unimpeded and variable settling and redirecting techniques and the situational use and pressure of time, complexity, and precision.

The *disadvantages* of *flat-pass play* should also be obvious:

- *Flat passes* as alibi passes without tactical purpose and necessary actions. This most often results in a game-impacting loss of time and speed.
- *Passing techniques* that cannot be applied variably, safely, precisely, and at a fast pace facilitate loss of possession. In practice or competition this usually results in
  a. no pressure being built up against the opponent,
  b. a player's playing direction becoming imprecise, and

c. the *timing to the ball* ("When must I play the ball?") possibly becoming uncertain.

■ After *flat-pass play* players often stop instead of immediately moving into new positions and offering renewed support ("Play and go!").

■ The teammate often receives the *flat pass* frontally. This eliminates some of his surprise playing options based on just his position relative to the ball: turns, starts, changes in direction.

■ Scenario: The team entrenches itself on one side of the field with *short passes*. The *opening, hard switch pass* does not follow.

■ One *flat pass* follows another, but no finishing actions take place.

Which drills and forms of play can be used to (selectively) emphasize *flat-passes* so that play can be positively impacted by the outlined advantages? The following 10 drills and forms of play can.

Bastian Schweinsteiger playing a flat pass

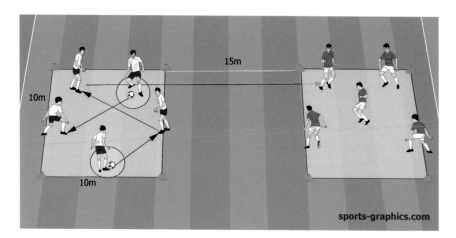

Fig. 59: Flat-pass play on two fields—two tactical passing squares

Organization:

- Five players in each of two passing squares (approximately 10 x 10 m).
- The five players in the two passing squares wear bibs of two different colors.
- The passing squares are marked at a 15 m distance.
- There are two balls in one square.

Progression:

- The players in one square pass the balls directly to each other.
- The coach or instructor specifies after several *combination passes* to play an opening ball to a player in the neighboring square.
- The passing player immediately switches to that square ("Play and Go!").
- The players in one square should not randomly position themselves. The coach or instructor will predetermine a specific strategic staggered formation.
- The coach or instructor issues additional tasks. Within each square, balls are always passed direct and flat.

Coaching:

- "Make sure passes are incisive!" (*Passing technique*)
- "Maintain the arranged order on the fields!" (*Passing tactics*)
- The *opening pass* must be purposeful.

Variations:

- Play with one ball.

- Increase or decrease the number of players.

- Contrast:

  1. *Play to the foot.*

  2. *Play into the running path.*

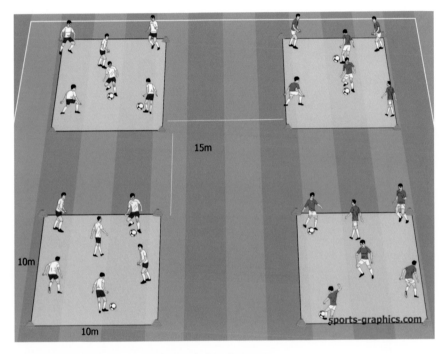

Fig. 60: Flat-pass play on four fields—four tactical passing squares

Organization:

- See fig. 59 in which four instead of two passing squares must be marked.

Progression:

- Now six players play in each square in a (tactical) 3v3 formation.

- The players independently control team play and make flat passes into the various squares without changing positions.

Coaching:

- "High passing speed must be maintained!" (*Passing technique*)
- "Frequently play the flat pass with the inside foot!" (*Passing technique*)
- Use both feet (*passing technique*).

Variations:

- Hold on to the ball: 3v3 in the squares.
- Use variations with the specified passing techniques (*passing technique and intelligence*).
- Play only *flat passes with the third man*.

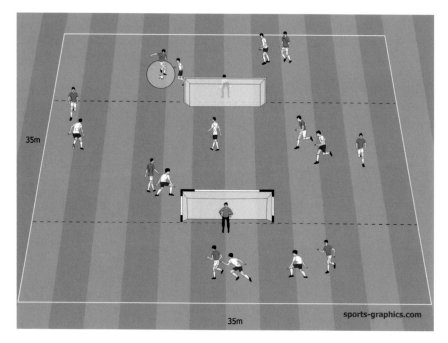

Fig. 61: Flat-pass soccer on four goals that have been turned around

Organization:

- A 35-x-35-m playing field is divided into three zones.
- The middle zone is larger than the other two zones.
- 8v8 at two goals that have been turned around, with goalies.

Progression:

- 4v4 in the middle zone.

- 2v2 in the two end zones.

- The players in the middle zone should develop and play the *killer pass* out of *flat passes*.

- The attackers in the end zone should get to the finish as quickly as possible; *flat passes* should also be used in this zone.

Coaching:

- "Our motto: If the passing path is blocked, we cut and shift play!" (*Passing philosophy*)

- "Let the ball do the work!" (*Passing technique*)

- "Create space without the ball!" (*Passing fitness*)

Variations:

- Play with only one touch in the middle.

- Use only one touch in the end zones to get to the finish.

- Whenever the ball is passed at waist height, the opposing team immediately gets a penalty kick.

Fig. 62: Flat passing in four zones

Organization:

- 11v11 at two large goals with goalies on a large field.
- Each half of the playing field is divided into two zones.

Progression:

- The ball can only be passed, not dribbled, from one zone to another.
- The final shot can only be taken from the last zone.
- Flat-pass play is mandatory for all players.

Coaching:

- "Continue to form triangles!" (*Passing tactics*)
- "Quickly play the opening pass!" (*Passing philosophy*)
- "Keep up the pace!" (*Passing philosophy*)

Variations:

- Only use one touch during buildup (*passing philosophy*).

- Play with one touch in the offensive half whenever possible (*passing philosophy*).
- Do not pass the ball back (*passing philosophy*).

THE CLOCK IS TICKING! FLAT-PASS PLAY IN FOUR ZONES

Organization: See fig. 62.

Progression:
- The clock is ticking, meaning there is time pressure with possession.
- Attackers must reach the next zone within 12 sec. This also applies to end zones with corresponding finishes.

Coaching:
- "Look forward!" (*Passing tactics and philosophy*)
- "Play deep!" (*Passing tactics and philosophy*)
- "Get out of the cover shadow!" (*Passing tactics and philosophy*)

Variations:
- Decrease duration.
- Decrease field size.
- Rule: A penalty kick is awarded whenever three waist-high or high balls have been played.

4.3.7 THE SHOT-AT-GOAL PASS

"To his colleagues who squander an opportunity in front of the goal Weidenfeller recommends to sometimes just blast the ball in. Like Götze did when he brilliantly accepted Müller's hard square pass and instinctively looked for the quickest solution to the finish that can't be found in any textbook."

(Frankfurter Allgemeine Zeitung, Nov. 25, 2013, 274, pg. 11).

A *shot-at-goal pass* is a purposeful pass at the opposing goal that is meant to lead to a goal. It is usually executed with very high velocity, whereby the push pass and the instep pass (see Bisanz and Gerisch 2013, pg. 332-363) *passing techniques* are the methods intended to result in a goal. In everyday soccer language, the *shot-at-goal* pass is also referred to as putting the ball in the back of the net!

The following fig. 63 shows the simulated situation of a fast dribble with subsequent *shot at goal* to one of the two players moving up (Brazil in white/blue) against the Netherlands (in red/white) on July 2, 2010, at the FIFA World Cup, with a 0-0 score (start of action at 7:12 minutes of playing time) (also see chapter 4.3.5 in conjunction with a *no-look pass*).

Fig. 63: Shot-at-goal pass after a no-look pass and fast dribble in the 2010 FIFA World Cup game Brazil vs. Netherlands

EXAMPLES FOR PRACTICE AND INSTRUCTION

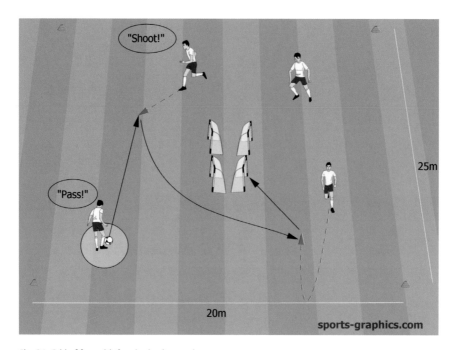

Fig. 64: Grid of four with four ice hockey goals

Organization:

- A field approximately 20 x 25 m, depending on the intent of the passes.
- Set up four cones at the far sides.
- Set up four ice hockey goals (mini goals) in the center of the field.

Progression:

- Four players practice together with quick (hard) passes in a grid of four.
- The players command each other to shoot for the *shot-at-goal* pass at one of the four ice hockey goals or pass to be ready to accept the ball because the pass is coming.
- If the shooter scores, he can immediately keep playing. If he misses he has to run a penalty lap (*passing fitness*). Have lots of balls available.

Coaching:

- All players are in a state of ball expectation.
- Ask for fast reaction with a *shot-at-goal pass*.
- "Decide!" If there is opportunity for an incisive and quick *shot-at-goal pass*, immediately take it.

Variations:

- Goals are moved farther apart, increasing the risk for the shooter.
- Players are behind the cones and must execute a feint (in front of the cone) prior to the *shot-at-goal* pass.
- The players play *lob passes* to each other and try to kick the ball directly into the goal from the air (volley).

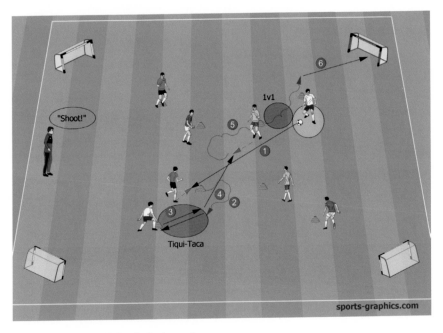

Fig. 65: Grid of eight with four ice hockey goals

Organization:

- A 40-x-45-m field, depending on the intent of the passes.
- Set up eight cones with one player stationed at each.

- Four ice hockey goals and four balls.
- The distance between each pair of cones and the ice hockey goals staggered behind them is approximately 5 m.
- Distance from cones to ice hockey goal is approximately 10 m.

Progression:

- At an agreed upon signal, the players of a player pair near the goal first pass the ball to the front player opposite them, who *settles the ball, turns away*, and immediately plays *Tiqui-Taca* with his partner.
- The coach watches the *Tiqui-Taca* and shouts out "Shoot!" The ball then once again goes to the front player of the opposite player pair, who *settles the ball, turns away*, and goes into an offensive 1v1 at the ice hockey goal until the finish.

Coaching:

- Keep up auditory and visual perception.
- Play quick and incisive passes and avoid collisions.
- The player who wins the 1v1 must immediately play the *shot-at-goal pass*.
- Mindset: Courage to take a risky shot-at-goal pass.

Variations:

- After the shoot signal, the player pairs open with a pass to the player pair to their left or right. Make specific agreements, demand synchronicity, avoid disorder.
- With the start of the 1v1, the players with the ball can also play at another goal. This forces them to play a longer *shot-at-goal pass*.
- As the players accept the pass after the code word "shoot," the opposing player runs toward the goal for the 1v1 and makes it smaller. Who will still get off a successful *shot-at-goal pass*? Hold competitions!
- Set up two large goals with goalies in the center of the playing field. The players can also choose to play offensive 1v1 against the goalie.
- Additional mini and large goals are set up behind the ice hockey goals at various distances on the field. The players with the ball can also play quick and incisive shots (*passes*) *at these goals*.
- Use fewer balls (reduce the high degree of difficulty).

Fig. 66: Shot-at-goal pass on goals that have been turned around

Organization:

- 9v9 at two large goals with goalies on one half of a playing field.
- Both large goals and goalies are turned around on the field.
- The playing field is divided into three vertical zones; the center zone takes up most of the field width.

Progression:

- 2v2 play takes place in each of the two outside zones, 5v5 in the middle zone.
- Only one or two touches are used in the middle zone.
- Open play 2v2 in the outside zones.
- The red team can only pass to their two red forwards to score. The playing direction is thereby predetermined.

Coaching:

- The two forwards should behave in such a way that they are immediately able to play the *shot-at-goal pass*.
- Players in the middle zone should only play the ball to the two forwards when it can also be played as a *shot-at-goal pass*, otherwise buildup preparation should continue.

159

- Whenever one forward accepts the ball, the other one must create space so the forward in possession can take the *shot-at-goal pass*.

Variations:

- Open play in the middle zone, and one to two touches in the outside zones.
- Play only ground passes, and the *shot-at-goal pass* must also be flat.
- 6v6 in the middle, and 1v1 in the two outside zones.

SHOT-AT-GOAL PASS WITH THE GOALS TURNED AROUND II

Organization: See fig. 66.

Progression:

See fig. 66 in which the four players in the outside zones can score with a *shot-at-goal pass.* This eliminates the obvious playing direction.

Coaching:

- The four players in the outside zones must now attack and defend.
- Whenever the goalie makes a save, the second ball must also be played as a *shot-at-goal pass.*
- Players without the ball should always get out of the opponent's *cover shadow*.

Variations:

- Whenever a *forward* gets possession, he must play an offensive 1v1.
- Forwards can only play flat *shot-at-goal passes.*
- If a forward's *shot-at-goal pass* misses the goal, he switches to the center (middle zone) and plays in the 6v5. If he scores in this zone with a *shot-at-goal pass,* he can continue to play with the superior numbers (*generate pressure*).

SHOT-AT-GOAL PASS WITH THE GOALS TURNED AROUND III

Organization: See fig. 66.

Progression:

See fig. 66 in which a player can move up and create superior numbers in the outside zone (offensive 3v2) after passing from the middle zone to a forward. A player in the vicinity of the passed ball can also move up (*anticipating situations*).

Coaching:

- "Don't get frantic during the offensive 3v2, but rather keep possession!"
- The *shot-at-goal pass* is taken after the gap has been detected.
- Try to fully use the small spaces in the outside zone. Motto: *"Spread out in small spaces!"*

Variations:

- If a forward moves up and creates superior numbers in the outside zone, a defender from the center can also move up. This creates a 3-on-3.
- If a forward moves up, but the defender can only move up into the outside zone after a 5 sec. delay—motto: "Incisively, confidently, and quickly take advantage of the small window of opportunity during superior numbers play (3v2)!"
- In a superior numbers situation, the *shot-at-goal pass* must be played after 5 sec. The coach also keeps time (see chapter 4.3.4 with the practice example from the Brazil vs. Netherlands game).

4.3.8 THE LAST-MOMENT PASS

"Thiago Alcántara do Nascimento caused ecstasy in this unique way when he dispatched a fascinating deep pass with a volley against Eintracht Frankfurt."

(Neue Nassauische Presse, Feb. 6, 2014, pg. 11).

Every soccer player and soccer fan is familiar with the situation when a mostly dribbling payer runs diagonally toward an opponent and fakes an offensive 1v1, but actually waits to play the pass until his opponent decides to tackle him, creates a passing gap for a deep flat pass into a teammate's running path, or a quick and incisive *shot-at-goal pass* can be taken near the goal (passing tactics).

Furthermore, the *last-moment pass* plays a central role in the game's transition phases by not playing the ball too soon but rather dribbling it through the space first so the opponent orients himself toward his own goal (cause the defenders to run back).

Principle: The more unimpeded a player can advance into the vicinity of the opposing goal, the wider the shooting angle to the large goal and the less time for effective reactions and anticipation. This advantage can also be increased by the possibly retreating goalie.

But there are also game situations where the player waits so long to take the pass that the opponent takes that one step forward. Until that moment, one teammate could usually have gotten open and could have been passed to or had a pass played into his running path, and the defender's opposite movement would not make a successful chase possible (*passing mindset*).

The following fig. 67 shows the simulated situation of dribbling toward the opposing central defender (here Pique in a back three) with the subsequent *last-moment pass* to the *crossing* forward van Persie (*arc*) (here Arsenal London in red/white) against FC Barcelona (here in white/blue) on Feb. 16, 2011, in the Champions League game, with a 0-0 score (start of action at 4:21 min. of playing time).

Fig. 67: Last-moment pass with crossing player van Persie in the Champions League game Arsenal London vs. FC Barcelona

EXAMPLES FOR PRACTICE AND INSTRUCTION

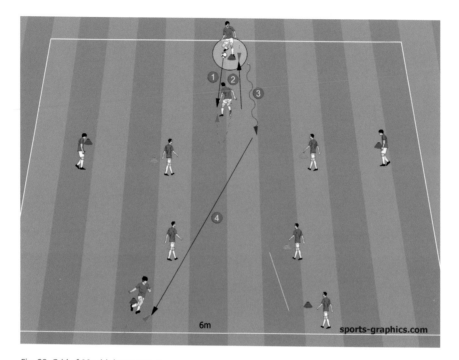

Fig. 68: Grid of 10 with last-moment passes

Organization:

- 10 cones are set up in a sort of circle of five.
- Of these, two cones (blue and red) always face each other approximately 6 m apart.
- One player per cone.
- Use one or several balls.
- Set distances according to training plan.

Progression:

- The player in the circle stands behind his blue cone and passes the ball to the player opposite him, who lets it *rebound*.
- The player dribbles past his blue cone and then dribbles on toward the player at the red cone.

- The player dribbles past him, or rather feints, and then passes the ball in the last second (*last-moment pass*) to an *off-the-ball* player.
- He settles the ball, turns away, and plays the same sequence again with the teammate at the blue cone.

Coaching:

- "Approach in a dribble as fast as possible and feint!"
- Keep the head up while dribbling and already think about which player to play the *last-moment pass* to.
- "Dribble approach and pass should not be hasty!"
- Use code words (see chapter 4.5).

Variations

- Don't dribble past the cone but rather toward the cone, then dribble back, and then pass.
- Specify certain feints and have the players use them.
- The player near the ball moves toward the dribbling player and tries to interfere with the passing path to the off-the-ball player. The player in possession must then decide if he should play the ball right away or in the last moment (*passing intelligence*).
- Playing several balls simultaneously can increase intensity and focus.
- Place dummies or large cones in the seams to make the incisive *last-moment pass* more difficult.
- Set up no-get-up-and-go goals at the sides. These can be quickly and incisively played at from time to time with a flat instep kick (motivation and contrast particularly with youth players: "Sometimes you have to rock the net!").

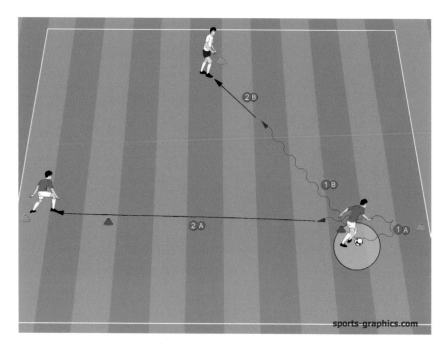

Fig. 69: Grid of three in individual last-moment mode

Organization:

Five cones, two of which stand closely side by side and one cone approximately 15 m to the side of the four cones.

Progression:

- One player stands at each of the cones standing side by side opposite him.
- The third player stands at the cone to the side.
- The player in the circle has the ball at his foot and can decide if he
  a. wants to dribble toward the cone near the ball and only then pass to the player opposite him standing at the pair of cones, or
  b. dribble toward the third player and then pass to him at the last moment.

If the third player receives the ball, he settles and controls it and dribbles toward the second player, and in the last moment plays a pass in front of him.

Coaching:

- "Practice as fast as possible!"
- "Use both feet to pass!"
- Demand lots of feints during dribble approach.

Variations:

- Increase distances between cones and ask for *chip* and *up-and-over balls*.
- Set up a goal with goalie behind the third player that he can move against and shoot at in the same mode after receiving the *last-moment pass*.
- The third player is the *rebounder*, so the other two players start a post-action immediately after their *last-moment pass* (passing fitness). The next action can then be initiated.

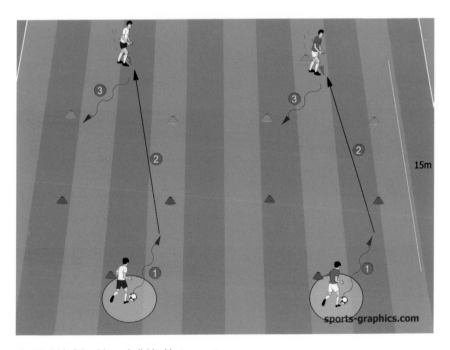

Fig. 70: Grid of six with two individual last-moment passes

Organization:

- Each player sets up his own cone triangle.
- The distance between cones can vary.

- The teammate stands opposite him at his cone triangle, approximately 15 m away.
- One ball per player pair.

Progression:

- The players stand with the ball at the tip of the cone triangle and dribble to one of the other cones in the triangle.
- The players dribble around just one cone and then
  a. pass the ball to the player on the opposite side or
  b. continue to dribble and at some point choose the *last-moment pass* to the teammate.
- With the *last-moment pass* from the passing player, the teammate decides if he wants to
  a. *make space* (stay off the ball) or
  b. start into the ball, *cut to the outside*, and then dribble the ball to his cones in the triangle.

Coaching:

- Take short, small dribble steps to the cones on the ball side and play *last moment-passes*.
- "Keep up the pace!"
- "Always stay quick on the ball!"

Variations:

- Only allow step-overs in the cone triangle (*ball control, feinting and passing technique*).
- Only allow Zidane moves in the cone triangle.
- "Don't dribble past the cone but rather pass when you are level with the two cones!"

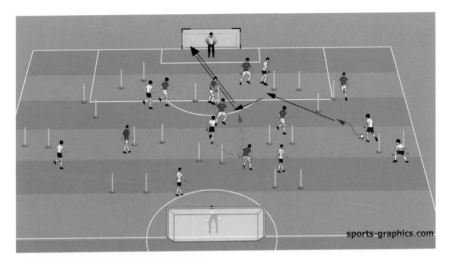

Fig. 71: 8v8 formation with last-moment cone goals

Organization:

- 8v8 at two large goals with goalies on one half of a large field.
- Set up 10 to 12 cone goals on the one half of a large field.

Progression:

- Players can only play with one to two touches or find one of the cone goals if they want to open dribble.
- Players cannot dribble through the cone goals but rather must pass the ball through the cone goals in the last moment. This is worth one point.
- If the pass reaches a teammate, it is worth an extra point.

Coaching:

- Foster the courage to approach with a dribble (*passing mindset*).
- Foster the courage to take the late pass (*passing mindset*).
- The player without the ball must execute *pre-actions*. (Motto: "Offer yourself for a possible pass!")

Variations:

- Now the ball must be dribbled through the cone goals.
- Dribble through the cone goals so that you come out exact and very tight against

the edge of the respective cone (left or right cone of the cone goal) at a fast pace.

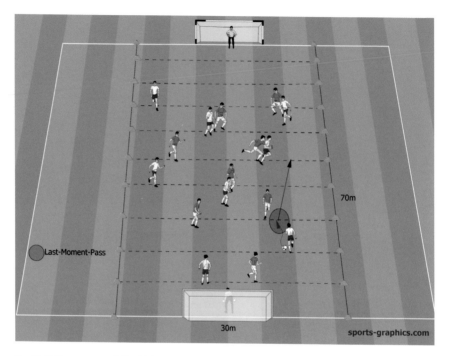

Fig. 72: 8v8 on a narrow field with last-moment zones

- **■** *Organization:*
- **■** 8v8 at two large goals with goalies on a playing field that is 70 x 30 m.
- **■** Mark 10 horizontal zones.
- **■** Possibly use colored marking tape.

Progression:

- **■** The players can only pass to another zone if they do it in the last moment before crossing into the next zone.
- **■** The players dribble through one zone but cannot dribble into the next zone. They must again pass into the next zone before crossing into it.
- **■** The players are now allowed to also play the *last-moment pass* through two zones (practice longer passes).

Coaching:

- "Form lots of triangles!"
- "Avoid square passes!"
- "Look and play deep!"

Variations:

- The players can only pass from zone to zone (*short passes*).
- The ball cannot be passed back.
- Shorten the length of the playing field and increase the width. Intent: Play wider passes (*passing philosophy*).

Fig. 73: Götze-Messi play (2v2)

Organization:

- 2v2 at two large goals with goalies on a playing field that is 25 x 50 m.

Progression:

- One player from each pair ("Messi") is allowed to only dribble and then must immediately take a shot at the opposing goal.

- The other player from each pair ("Götze") is also allowed to only dribble, but not during the tactical 1v1 on offense; rather "Götze" always uses the *last-moment pass* to pass to "Messi" (*passing tactics*).

Coaching:

- Always keep up the pace on the ball.

- "Götze" must give "Messi" the open *space* for a fast dribble with subsequent finish.

- "Messi" must always get out of the cover shadow so that "Götze" can play the *last-moment pass*.

Variations:

- When "Messi" is unable to take a shot, he is allowed to stop dribbling and pass to "Götze" (*passing tactics*).

- Create time pressure: Shot must be taken within 6 sec.

- Add a neutral player to create 3v2 in which the neutral player can only play one touch.

11V11 WITH FOUR MANDATORY TOUCHES

Organization:

- 11v11 at two large goals with goalies on a large field.

Progression:

- Each player, except the goalie, must play four mandatory touches.

- The ball can only be passed to the teammate after the third touch.

Coaching:

- Don't just quickly touch the ball consecutively, but rather use the four mandatory touches to create open space with it (*passing tactics*).

- Use a fast dribble approach and pass in the last moment.

- Alternate between fast dribble and ball control while dribbling.

Variations:

- Play a *wall pass* as the *last-moment pass.*
- If the *last-moment pass* is a *killer pass* and results in a goal, the player without the ball may also use only one touch for the finish.
- The ball can only be played forward or to the side.

4.3.9 THE KILLER PASS

> *"And yet during the confusion and fog of battle, there were also those who seemed to be guided ... directed ...seeing something, someone ... others couldn't see."*
>
> (Gary Beikirh)

The chosen term has nothing to do with the duel to the death. The *killer pass* is merely a term for the pass into the last zone, the *danger zone*, before the goal. When a player gets an unimpeded finish in this zone, it is often an indicator for a team's success. [13]Accordingly, the pass into this zone, in keeping with soccer lingo, can be deadly.

Statistically, playing through the center is almost always done vertically with the help of a *killer pass* (playing deep). This pass is highly demanding in terms of technical and tactical abilities and skills, especially considering the center is usually compressed by numerous attacking opponents. The huge amount of pressure on the ball and the *blocked passing lanes* present a major challenge for the players (*passing technique and tactics*). Therefore players in possession should learn by using many applicable drills and forms of play to

---

14 *The editorial department at the trade magazine fussballtraining (Soccer Training) (2013, pg. 6-7) was able to work out that one-third of all goals scored on set plays at the 2012 European Championships came from passes through the center or up-and-over passes.*

- stay calm in front of the goal in spite of the huge amount of stress (*passing mindset*),
- estimate your own timing as well as the amount of time needed to the running path of the player without the ball (*passing intelligence*), and
- choose the right passing technique.

The following fig. 74 shows the simulated situation of Xavi's *flat pass* with the outside of the foot (white/blue) through the center of the midfield (skipping one line) to the 9er, who lets the ball rebound to the 10er, here Messi (white/blue), who then plays the *killer pass* just past the opposing central defender (red/white) and into the last zone. This solution to the game situation is also *play with the third man*. Arsenal London (red/white) against FC Barcelona (white/blue) in the Feb. 2, 2011 Champions League game with a score of 0-0 (action sequence with times: 14:19 to 14:22 minutes of playing time).

Fig. 74: Killer pass into the danger zone in the context of a play with a third man in the Arsenal London vs. FC Barcelona Champions League game

Of importance is that the entire passing combination up to the fast dribble in the danger zone lasts only 3 seconds.

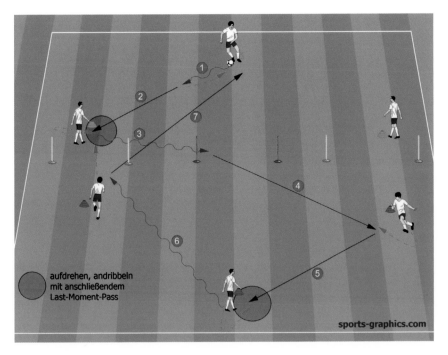

Fig. 75: Two grids of three (with point in the back) with pole goals in the center and offensive play

Organization:

- Set up three cones in a triangle formation with a distance of approximately 8m.
- Place three pole goals in between these two triangle formations.
- The geometry is specified as *point in the back*.

Progression:

In the *triangle formation* (with point in the back!), the player with the ball is attacked by the player at the blue cone, who is supposed to prevent the *killer pass* or make it more difficult (competition-related).

Coaching:

- "Try to immediately get in the *open position*!"

- "Too late? Focus on playing with the opponent at your back!"

- "Play incisive passes at the end of the combination!"

Variations:

- Every *killer pass* is awarded one point (competition).

- Every successful defense against a *killer pass* is awarded one point (competition).

- Increase distances to each other, allowing the players to develop a 3v3.

Fig. 76: 6v6 plus 4 on a tight field

Organization:

- 6v6 at two large goals with goalies on a 40-x-25-m playing field (tight field).

- Behind each of the two goals are two passing players from the attacking team.

Progression:

- 6v6 in a narrow corridor in which the players on the field must look for the deep killer pass (*passing intelligence*).
- Looking for and finding the deep *killer pass* should also involve the two wingers who can bring the ball back into play with merely *one touch*.

Coaching:

- "Incisive and hard passes toward the passing player."
- "Quick and hard combinations among yourselves!"
- "In a tight space quickly break away and use body feints!"

Variations:

- The width of the playing field is decreased.
- The teams play with two mandatory touches.
- Every passing player (with ball) must continue to find another teammate.
- The passing players stand on the field (*Barcelona-style*).

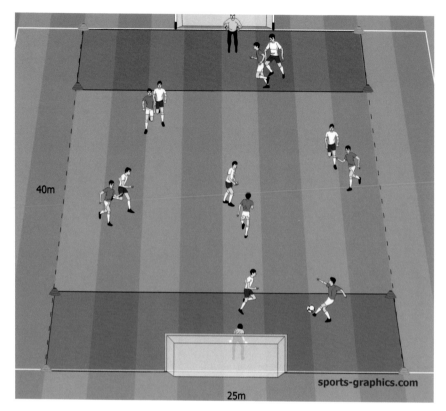

Fig. 77: From 6v6 to double 1v1 pairs

Organization:

- See fig. 76 in which only two attack zones are marked in front of the two goals, where one *1v1 pair* is positioned.
- The tight corridor remains in place to continue to encourage the players to play long balls.

Progression:

- Starting position: 6v6 in the middle zone.
- The two teams must try to pass to the striker in the respective attack zone.
- The two attackers must use individual and group tactics to break away from the two defenders; they should be able to receive the long ball and score a goal.

Coaching:

- "Don't rush the *killer pass*!"
- Avoid waist-high *killer passes* to the two attackers because this makes it difficult to settle the ball.
- Depending on the situation, the two attackers can also hold and shield the ball and then pass it to the midfielders who are moving up.

Variations:

- Only the two attackers are allowed to score goals.
- Both attack zones are enlarged so that a 2v2 can be played there. The two attackers play with just one touch, so they can take a direct shot at goal.

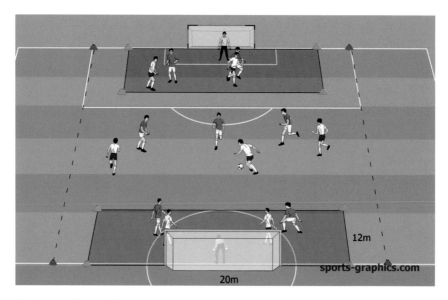

Fig. 78: 7v7 with deep ball at 2v2 attack zones

Organization:

- 7v7 at two large goals with goalies on one half of a large field.
- Set up a 20-x-12-m attack zone in front of the two goals in which two attackers play against two defenders.
- The wings remain open.

Progression:

- The seven *midfielders* must place the two respective attackers in effective goal-scoring settings with the help of the *killer pass*.

Coaching:

- Keep an eye on the running paths of the two attackers (e.g., one is coming, the other one is going). Objective: To make *space* for the *killer pass*.
- Break off when the *killer pass* does not fit the game situation. Start a new buildup.
- Play the killer pass slightly to the side of the teammate.

Variations:

- 2v1 or 1v1 in the respective attack zone.

- When the attacker is able to successfully finish the *killer pass* at the goal with one touch, the goal is worth three points. Possibly develop this into a competition with a chart to further increase motivation, or let the players develop it (*passing mindset*).

- After a successful long pass, the midfielders are allowed to move into the attack zone to create superior numbers (*increase pressure of complexity*).

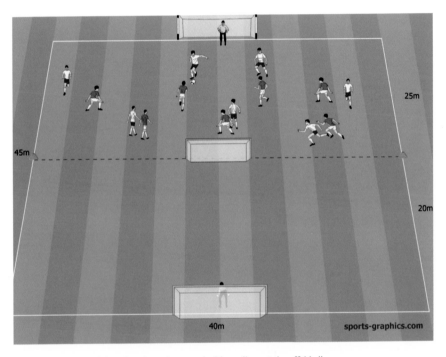

Fig. 79: 7v7 at the mini goal and at a large goal with goalie past the offside line

Organization:

- 7v7 on a playing field that is 45 x 40 m.
- The *first zone* extends from one large goal with goalie to the mini goal and is 25 m deep.
- The *second zone* extends from the mini goal (depending on level of play) to the large goal with goalie and is 20 m deep.
- The byline at a level with the mini goal is the offside line.

Progression:

- 7v7 at the mini goal in which a goal is scored when the ball touches the goal net directly.

- A goal is also scored when the long ball is played before the offside line (*killer pass*), and the player receiving the pass controls it and dribbles alone toward the large goal with goalie.

- If the *killer pass* is played before the offside line, the finish at the large goal is worth three points.

Coaching:

- The fast and perfectly-timed *killer pass* must be played out of the narrow space.

- The receiving players must make sure they are not offside.

- Use the *chip ball* as a passing alternative to the *killer pass*.

Variations:

- 7v7 in front of the mini goal playing with *one touch* only.

- Increase field size to make studying the running paths easier.

- Exchange the mini goal for a large goal with goalie.

Fig. 80: 11v11 with killer passing zones

Organization:

- 11v11 on a three-quarter field with two large goals and goalies.

Progression:

- The penalty box dimensions are mirrored at the 16 m lines and marked respectively as zones (here in blue).
- A goal can only be scored when a *killer pass* is played into these zones.

Coaching:

- Dribble around the blocked passing lanes.
- Do *not* play the ball directly in front of the forward's feet.
- Moreover, also look for and play the *pass into an open space* to make the forward run.

Variations:

- If the *killer pass* into the zone in front of the goal is not possible, dribble alone into the last zone and finish (*passing tactics and intelligence*).
- The killer pass can only be played as a ground pass (*passing technique*).
- Expand the playing field to the entire large field (*passing fitness*).

4.3.10 THE UP-AND-OVER PASS

"Young players need freedom of expression to develop as creative players [...] They should be encouraged to try without fear of failure."

(Arsène Wenger—FC Arsenal London).

Speculating about passing play in general usually requires thinking exclusively about *flat-pass* and *short-pass play* for practice and competition. Coaches and instructors mostly think about combining them and playing together.

But as was already established with the *killer pass* and the implied chip ball[14], it is statistically significant that many goals in today's professional soccer are scored after a pass up and over the defense (see *fussballtraining* 2013, pg. 6-7). Why is this becoming more common in a game? Nowadays many defenses play relatively high lines. That means they

a.   want to get the ball in the first *line*, and

b.   keep the opponent far away from the goal.

For these reasons an incisive up-and-over chip ball played from a midfield position—this defensive position is usually referred to as the *last line*—is very effective. The space behind the last line can only be directly defended by the goalie. It therefore makes a lot of sense to think about practicing *up-and-over passes* during training.

The following fig. 81 shows the simulated situation of a diagonal *flat pass* from a 6er out of the right halfback position in the opposing half (white/blue) through the center

---

14   *We use the conceptual pair chip ball, which is used very frequently in everyday practice, in part synonymously for the up-and-over puzzle designation.*

to the left toward the approaching 8er (from left halfback position; white/blue), who plays an *up-and-over pass* over the central defender (red/white) who has moved up and is blocking the direct ground passing lane to the 9er in the center (white/blue) and in behind the defense. This scene stems from the Atletico Madrid (red/white) vs. Atletico Bilbao (white/blue) game on May 9, 2012, in the European League final with a 0-0 score (action sequence with times: 05:00 to 05:02 of playing time).

Fig. 81: The up-and-over pass into the danger zone in the 2012 European League final between Atletico Madrid and Atletico Bilbao

Here, too, we must point out the very brief time period (approximately 3 sec.) between the diagonal *flat pass* and the *up-and-over pass* until the finish.

EXAMPLES FOR PRACTICE AND INSTRUCTION

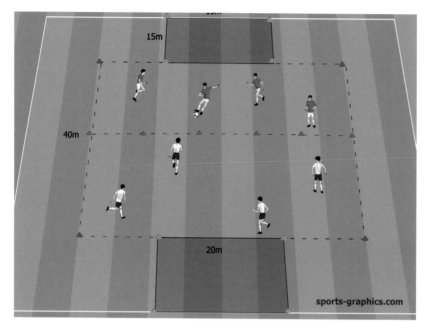

Fig. 82: Up-and-over soccer tennis

Organization:

- 4v4 soccer tennis on a playing field that is 40 x 20 m.
- The field is divided in half by a centerline.
- A 15-x-15-m zone (end zone) is added behind each end of the field.

Progression:

- Rules: Only one point can be scored at any time. Exception: The ball is chipped over the four players in either end zone. Then the team is awarded five points.
- Players must not stay in the end zones.
- If the ball is played into an end zone, the players can run there, control the ball, and try to keep the ball within their ranks.
- Adjust the degree of difficulty according to the team's playing level. That means:
  a. only volley touches,
  b. only one touch on the ground per team, and
  c. variations after verbal agreement.

Coaching:

- Continuously ask for the courage to take the chip pass (*passing mindset*).
- Don't rush the ball into the end zones.
- If the game doesn't permit, just hold the ball within your ranks (*passing intelligence and tactics*).

Variations:

- The field is enlarged considerably to increase the players' running performance (*passing fitness*).
- If the *up-and-over pass* is successful, it is worth an extra point.
- The ball can only be chipped into the end zone with a specific foot.

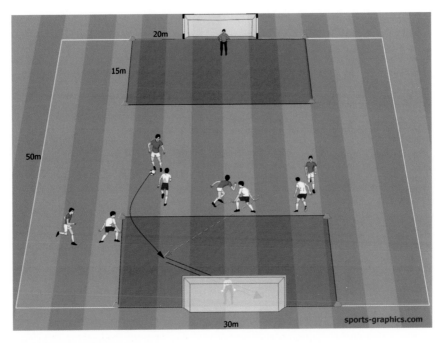

Fig. 83: 4v4 with end zones

Organization:

- 4v4 at two large goals with goalies on a playing field that is 50 x 30 m.
- A 20-x-15-m end zone is added in front of each goal.

Progression:

- Open play.
- The players can only score if the ball was first chipped into an end zone.

Coaching:

- Don't rush to play the last pass.
- Players can also play the *second ball* up and over.
- The goalie can then pass the ball into the end zone if the opposing defensive line is too high (*passing philosophy*).

Variations:

- Play with only one to two touches.
- Direct shot at goal from the end zone (*passing mindset*).
- Increase the length of the field so the *up-and-over passes* must be played from the behind.

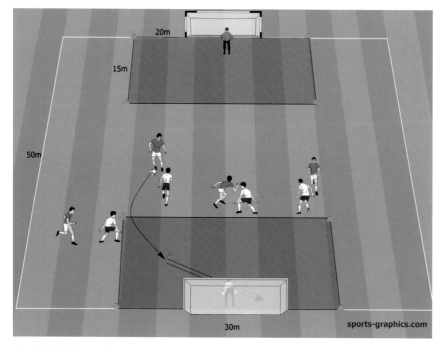

Fig. 84: 7v7 with up-and-over zones

Organization:

- 7v7 at two large goals with goalies on a playing field that is 70 x 50 m.
- An end zone is marked in front of each of the large goals.

Progression:

- Open play.
- All players play on the field only (without the end zones).
- A goal can only be scored if the ball is *chipped* over the *central 7v7 players*.
- When a forward runs into an end zone while watching the ball and is not offside, the defending team can no longer pursue him.

Coaching:

- The *up-and-over pass* must be played high above the last defender.
- The forwards start to run even though the *up-and-over pass* hasn't been played yet (*pre-actions, passing fitness*).
- "Be aware of the offside position!"

Variations:

- One defender is also allowed to run into the end zone after the *up-and-over pass*.
- The *killer (ground) pass* is also permitted.
- After the *up-and-over pass*, the ball must be kicked out of the air (volley) into the goal (*very demanding passing technique*).

Fig. 85: 8v5—short passes against up-and-over passes

Organization:

- 8v5 at two large goals with goalies on a playing field that is 60 x 40 m.

Progression:

- The superior numbers team can only play one to two touches.
- Players can play only *flat* and *combination passes* (*passing technique*).
- The team of five must chip the ball over the superior numbers team as quickly as possible and unnerve the superior numbers team with lots of *up-and-over passes* and disrupt the flow of their combinations—in other words, provocation (*passing mindset and philosophy*).

Coaching:

- One of the attackers on the outnumbered team must continue to start in the direction of the end zone (*passing fitness*).
- Play the chip balls incisively and without being rushed (*passing technique and mindset*).
- Play the *up-and-over passes* through the seams (*passing tactics*).

Variations:

- Change the number of players on the two teams.
- When the opposing goalie stops an *up-and-over ball*, he is awarded one point.
- Play with specific end zones where no defender from the superior number team is allowed to defend.

4.3.11 THE GIVE-AND-GO PASS AND BOUNCING

"More touches of the ball, more involvement in the game."

(Sir Alex Ferguson—Manchester United)

During competitive play, a player often receives a pass with the opponent at his back. Often the objective of this type of pass is

- to create a new geometry via the return pass,
- to gain time,
- to continue to move the own team up toward the opposing goal, and
- to pass the ball while under pressure from the opponent and subsequently get open.

From the point of view of the player who uses the *give-and-go pass* and *bouncing* (see chapter 4.3.2 on the *triangle pass*), these passes most often

- are played with one touch and a high passing rate,
- are *bounced* backward (e.g., the 9er with his back to the opponent),
- are played directly due to pressure from the opponent—*give* (pass)—*go* (return pass), and

- are passed directly into various directions and are linked to the search for a new running position (*rebound*).

In today's modern soccer, *give-and-go passes* and *bouncing* are frequently used in motion sequences and allow the midfielders and wingbacks in particular to move and turn more easily, confidently, and precisely on the turf.

This chosen terminology is intended to appeal to the players, especially on an emotional level. Players (and coaches and instructors) grinning and delighting in the choice of verbal images and borrowed metaphors in terms of knowledge and learning is expressly desired (see chapters 1 and 3).

The following fig. 86 shows the simulated situation of a *give-and-go pass* (white/blue) with subsequent *rebound* (bounce) (white/blue), *one-touch triangle pass*, and *switch pass* (white/blue) in the opposing half, from the right halfback position to the left wing (11er, white/blue). This scenario originates from the Brazil (here in white/blue) vs. the Netherlands (here in red/white) game from July 2, 2010, at the South Africa World Cup, with a 0-0 score (action sequence with times: 05:36 to 05:41 minutes playing time).

Fig. 86: Give-and-go pass, rebound, and the search for a new running position on the wing during the 2010 FIFA World Cup game Brazil vs. Netherlands

The search for a new and promising running position on the left wing with two *give-and-go passes*, subsequent rebound, followed by the *one-touch triangle pass* and the *switch pass* lasted only 5 sec.

EXAMPLES FOR PRACTICE AND INSTRUCTION

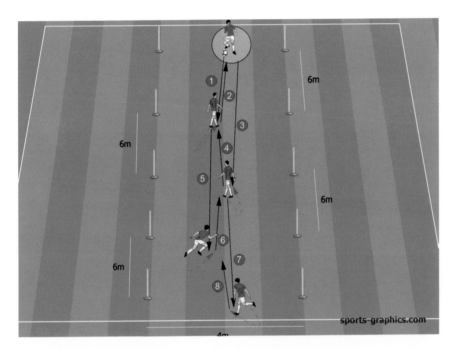

Fig. 87: Grid of five with rebound goals

Organization:

- Mark five cone goals that are approximately 4 m wide.
- The five cone goals are approximately 6 m apart.

Progression:

- One player is positioned in each cone goal.
- The player in the first cone goal plays the ball to the second player, who lets the ball *rebound*, after which the first player plays the ball on to the third player, and so on.
- After the *rebound* the player must immediately turn and pass the ball.

Coaching:

- Play the ball to the sides of the feet.

- Get into the ready position (ball anticipation position).

- *Rebound* without much rotation or spin on the ball.

Variations:

- Play only with the right foot.

- Play only with the left foot.

- The ball is only played high.

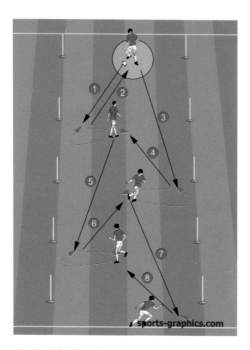

Fig. 88: Grid of five with rebound goals and lateral movement

Organization: See fig. 87.

Progression:

See fig. 87 in which the players without a ball offer the passing player an angle, meaning that they run to a cone, and the ball is passed to them from the left or right halfback position.

Coaching:

- Short run up to a cone.
- "Eyes on the ball!"
- Quick lateral steps; don't crisscross (*passing fitness*).

Variations:

- The passing player can play the ball anywhere, and all players must make their moves.
- The passing player puts the ball in the middle of the goal, and the second player should first feint to the outside and only after that quickly start back to the middle (*passing fitness*).
- No special running movements; the ball is *rebounded* (bounced) diagonally.

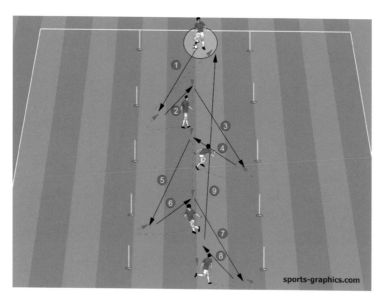

Fig. 89: Grid of five with rebound goals and position changes

Organization: See fig. 87.

Progression:

- The passing player passes the ball to the second player, who lets it *rebound*.
- The passing player continues to run through and plays the *rebounded* ball to the third payer out of the forward movement, and so on.
- When the passing player arrives at the last cone goal, he plays the ball back to the second player, who has by now assumed the position of passing player.

Coaching:

- The passing player cannot follow too quickly but instead must let the ball do its work (timing) (*passing technique*).
- "Always offer an angle!"
- The ball should not bounce; first choice is ground passes!" (*Passing technique*)

Variations:

- Play with specific feet.
- *Bounce the ball back* using the sole of the foot (*passing technique*).
- Practice with two touches.

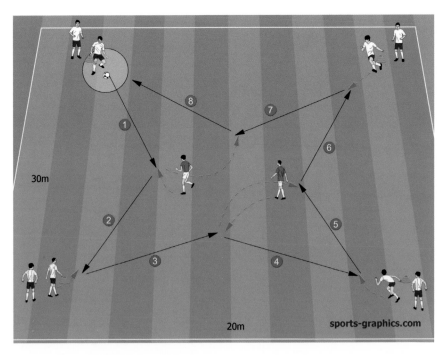

Fig. 90: Grid of four with rebounders in the center

Organization:

- Mark a 30-x-40-m square.

Progression:

- There is a player positioned at each cone (plus a supplementary player).
- There are two extra players in the middle.
- The passing player in the circle passes to the player closest to the ball in the center. He lets the ball rebound to the second outside player. The outside player plays the ball to the far player in the center who *rebounds* it to the third outside player, who then lets the ball *rebound* to the near player in the center. This player lets the ball *rebound* to the fourth outside player, and so on.

Coaching:

- If the ball is played too slowly, move toward the ball (*passing mindset*).
- If the ball is played too fast, chill for a moment.
- Always use *ground passes* (*passing technique*).

Variations:

- Pass and *rebound* using a specific foot.

- Play the ball waist-high and then *rebound* (*passing technique*).

- Ask for position changes all over (*passing tactics*).

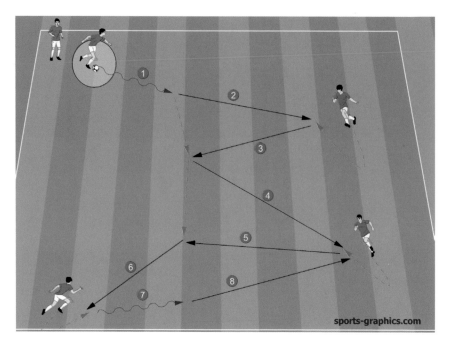

Fig. 91: Grid of four with running rebounder

Organization:

- Set up four cones on a field that is 40 x 15 m.

Progression:

- The player in the circle plays a diagonal pass to the player opposite him and then continues to run straight ahead. He receives the *rebounded* ball into his running path, passes it again diagonally to the next player, and keeps running forward. Then he receives a second *rebounded* pass into this running path. He then passes this ball straight ahead to the fourth player who briefly stops the sequence and then starts a new sequence (mirror reverse).

Coaching:

- All of the players are moving.
- "Ask for the ball!"
- "Fast pace!"

Variations:

- Practice with two *mandatory touches* (*passing technique*).
- Deliberately *pass* and *rebound* the ball behind the teammate to briefly halt team play (and be able to stand), much like a play-stop (*passing tactics*).
- Combine the sequence with a transition to the finish: One large goal with goalie off the marked field.
- Synchronization: When the first player goes, the second player *comes*. When the first player *rebounds*, the second player goes, and the third player comes (*coming and going in a group*).

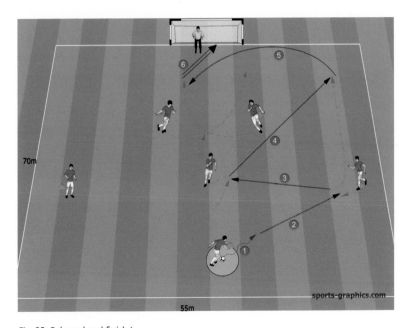

Fig. 92: Rebound and finish I

Organization:

- A 70-x-55-m playing field with a large goal and a goalie.

Progression:

- The player in the circle passes the ball to the right wing player.
- The wing player rebounds the ball to the center player, who then plays it into the running path of the wing player (*give-and-go passes*).
- The wing player passes/crosses the ball to the *intersecting* forwards or plays a hard (back) *ground pass* to the central player who is moving up.
- Change sides to start a new sequence.

Coaching:

- Precise running action (intersecting, moving up) to clear *passing lines* (*passing tactics and technique*).
- The wing player must run between the lines.
- To the *rebounders*: "Remember our motto: *Play and go!*"

Variations:

- The wing player plays a direct *wall pass* with the forward closer to the ball (*passing tactics*).
- The wing payer *rebounds* the ball to the passing player who turns to the other side and *rebounds* the ball to the other wing player (*passing technique*).
- The wing player passes the ball to a forward in the center who *rebounds* the ball to the previous passing player who is farther away and who then makes an opening pass to the other side to be played on the other wing (*passing tactics*).

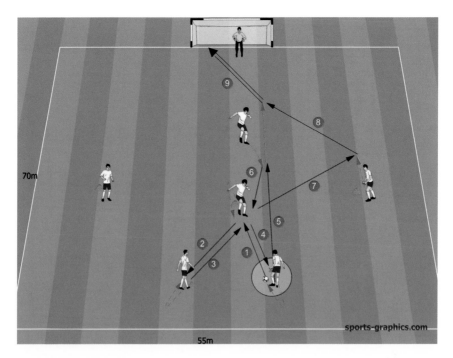

Fig. 93: Rebound and finish II

Organization: See fig. 92.

Progression:

- All players stand approximately in the center of one half of the playing field.
- Three players form a triangle as central *midfielders*.
- The player closest to the goal represents the *center forward*.
- The two outside players represent the *wing players*.
- The central midfielders play direct *triangle passes* to each other.
- The right central midfielder (6er) then plays a fake pass to the center forward (9er) who lets the ball *rebound* to the top of the triangle to the 10er.
- The 10er *rebounds* (in this case, opens) the ball to the right wing player, the 7er, who lets the ball *rebound* to the diagonally forward-running 9er.

Coaching:

- The midfielders stay connected.

- The 9er must *rebound* and *go*.
- The far *wing player* must play *second forward*.

Variations:

- The 6er plays the ball directly to the 9er.
- The 6er opens with a direct ball to the wing player who lets it *rebound* into the center.
- The 6er passes to the 9er. The 9er passes to the 10er who plays a *switch pass* to the wing player. This player *rebounds* with the 9er, and the wing forward plays a cross to the wing forward who is moving up and plays the finish.

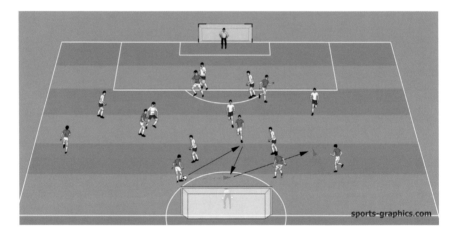

Fig. 94: 8v8 with rebounders

Organization:

- 8v8 at two large goals with goalies on one half of a large playing field.

Progression:

- When the ball is passed from one player to a teammate, he has to return the ball with a *rebound* (*give-and-go pass*).
- Only then can the player play the opening pass.

Coaching:

- Try not to close the space when rebounding.

- Play the short passes as hard *ground passes* (*passing technique*).
- When two players play together, a third player forms the triangle (*passing tactics*).

Variations:

- Play with one to two touches.
- Players without the ball must play in the open position.
- Narrow the playing field.

8V8 WITH REBOUND END ZONES

Organization: See fig. 94.

Progression:

- See fig. 94 in which a goal can only be scored if a forward is positioned in the end zone and *rebounds* the ball.
- A midfielder who is moving up takes a shot or plays the *killer pass* to the forward.

Coaching:

- Players must offer angles everywhere (*passing tactics*).
- Play incisive and quick passes (*passing technique*).
- Players without the ball must ask for the ball (*passing fitness*).

Variations:

- The forward is allowed to score when he does a *1v1 offensive* dribble.
- Players can play unrestricted but must *rebound* in the end zones.
- Narrow the playing field so the *rebounding element* (and the *give-and-go passes*) will be used much more frequently.

4.3.12 THE WALL PASS

"If World Player of the Year was an award for the most valuable player, meaning not his market value, but the value of his inner stability, overall strength, the magical togetherness of a team – then surely Ribéry would have been a better choice than Ronaldo, soccer's perfect scoring machine."

(Frankfurter Allgemeine Zeitung, Jan. 1, 2014, No. 11, pg. 23)

The *wall pass* is double the fun! Which soccer player isn't familiar with this saying? It points to the basic element of team play, playing with a teammate.

During a *wall pass*, a player is in possession and uses a *wall player* to have the ball returned to him. Thus the *wall pass* is a means for

- quickly regaining possession and
- quickly bridging a space.

In this context, the player in possession must pass the ball so that

- the wall player can pass it into a space or
- back to the passing player's foot for the *wall pass*.

In a competitive game, it often happens that two players on a team doing a quick passing combination outplay a player with a *wall pass*. For example, during the 2011/2012 Champions League season, 345 goals were scored, 29 of those with the aid of the *wall pass* and the *three-way combination* from combination play. The *wall pass* thus ranks fourth in the historical ranking of goals from open play (comparison: 39 goals from long shots; see UEFA 2012a, pg. 10).

If in this regard, training is supposed to also be effective for the success of (team) play. The coaches and instructors must design drills and forms of play that show the players running paths without the ball and also challenge the wall players to use only one touch.

The following fig. 95 shows the simulated situation of a wall pass by Arsenal London (red/white) on the left wing in their own half. The scene stems from the Arsenal London (red/white) vs. FC Barcelona (white/blue) Champions League game on Feb. 16, 2011, with a 0-0 score (action sequence with times: 04:13 to 04:15 of playing time).

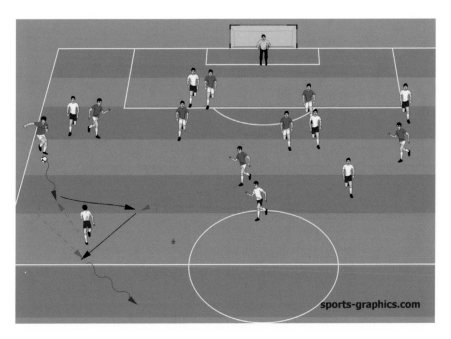

Fig. 95: Wall pass on the wing in the Champions League game Arsenal London vs. FC Barcelona

The ascertained time of 3 sec for possession, switch pass, and renewed possession shows how quickly a space can be bridged.

EXAMPLES FOR PRACTICE AND INSTRUCTION

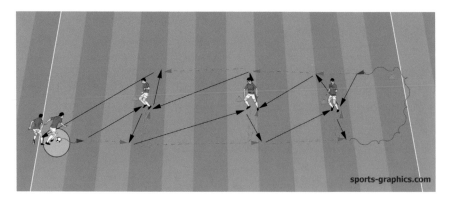

sports-graphics.com

Fig. 96: Grid of four with alternating wall passes

Organization:

- Five cones are set up slightly off-center in a line.
- One player per cone (four total).
- Freely choose the distances between cones based on skill level and training objectives.

Progression:

- The player in the circle plays the ball past the cone to the right or left foot of the teammate standing behind the second cone.
- He lets the ball *rebound* to the trailing player.
- He passes the ball to the next teammate.
- After the third *wall pass* to the players at the cones, the player settles the ball, turns around the fifth cone, and again plays three *wall passes* on the other side.
- The three wall players position so they can again let the ball *rebound* behind the cones.

Coaching:

- The player in the circle must configure his running paths so that he can change the *pace*. In doing so he must make sure he doesn't run too fast or too slow (*passing tactics*).

- The three *wall players* should be in the open position (*passing technique*).

- Play the ball as an incisive *ground pass* into the player's path (*passing technique*).

- If possible, do not play the pass with the *weak foot* (*passing technique*).

Variations:

- The wall player plays with two touches.

- The running player plays with two touches.

- The running player plays only one *wall pass sequence* and then passes a long ball directly to the first wall player. All other players move up to the next position.

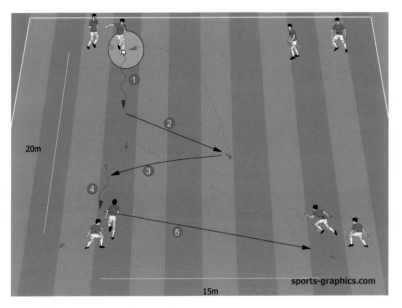

Fig. 97: Grid of four with quick wall passes

Organization:

Four players plus one supplemental player practice in a 20-x-15-m square.

Progression:

- The player in the circle approaches with a dribble and plays the ball to the teammate diagonally opposite him. As he begins his dribble, the player directly across from him attacks.

- This turns into a *wall pass* followed by settling the ball and another brief dribble approach.
- After that the player in possession makes a *diagonal* pass in the direction of the wall player's point of origin. But he can also forgo the pass and occupy the position of the teammate directly opposite him.
- The wall player and the defender look for another position.
- A new sequence begins in front of the new cone.

Coaching:

- Play hard passes (*passing technique*).
- The wall player plays the ball into the path.
- Don't lose track of the situation during the fast *dribble* (*passing intelligence*).

Variations:

- The player in the circle makes a *direct* pass to the player diagonally opposite him.
- The players play the *double-wall* pass, meaning the player in the circle executes two actions.
- The defending player tries to gain possession in the 2v1 situation and immediately after winning the ball plays a *wall pass* with a player positioned at one of the cones.

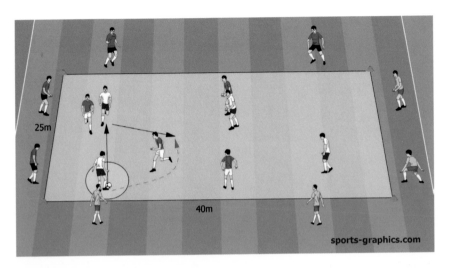

Fig. 98: 4v4 plus 8

Organization:

- 4v4 on a playing filed that is 40 x 25 m.
- Eight teammates stand evenly spread out at the edges of the field.

Progression:

- Open play.
- *Wall passes* played on the field or with the aid of the eight players are worth one bonus point for the respective team.
- After 60 sec of exertion, the players on the field switch with those off the field (*passing fitness*).

Coaching:

- Stay in possession.
- Do not play hasty wall passes (*passing tactics*).
- Don't constrict the space too frequently (*passing intelligence*).
- Always look for the *third man* (*passing tactics*).

Variations:

- Change field size (large vs. small).
- Execute only one to two touches on the field.

- *Wall passes* can only be played on the field, and the players at the edges of the field can only make opening passes to calm down the game (*passing mindset and tactics*).

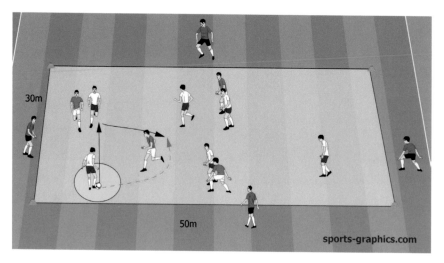

Fig. 99: 6v4 plus 4

Organization:

- 6v4 on a playing filed that is 50 x 30 m.
- Four players off the field play with the outnumbered team.

Progression:

- The superior numbers team plays with only one to two touches and must try to keep the ball in their own ranks.
- The outnumbered team must also try to keep the ball in their own ranks with the aid of the players at the edges of the field.
- Every team that plays a *wall pass* gets five bonus points.

Coaching:

- The outnumbered team must use the entire field during possession (*passing intelligence*).
- The wall player must let the ball rebound hard and with precision (*passing technique*).
- Create a situation on the field that facilitates fast play with a superior number.

Variations:

- 8v4 on the field, and the eight players play with only one touch.
- The players at the edges of the field play with the team in possession.
- *Wall passes* can only be played on the field, and the four players at the edges of the field can only look for the third man.

Fig. 100: 5v5 plus 4 with wall pass and finish

Organization:

- 5v5 at two large goals with goalies on a playing field that is 45 x 30 m.
- Four neutral players who must act as wall players are positioned behind the two goals.

Progression:

- 5v5 in which only one to two touches can be used on the field.
- The four neutral players play with just one touch and can only let the ball rebound to the player from whom they received it.

Coaching:

- After making a pass, the player with the ball must execute a specific running path to reach the wall pass (*passing fitness*).
- The wall player must be in the ready-to-receive position.
- If the situation doesn't allow for the *wall pass* to be played, the wall player must break off and *reopen* the game (*passing intelligence*).

Variations:

■ Open play.

■ The neutral players can also be positioned at the sides of the field.

■ The shot at goal must come immediately after the *wall pass*.

Fig. 101: 6v6 at two large goals with goalies on a 60-x-40-m playing field

Organization:

■ 6v6 at two large goals with goalies on a playing field that is 60 x 40 m.

Progression:

■ Open play.

■ Four neutral players are added at the two sides of the field. They will act as *wall players*.

■ *Wall passes* are worth five bonus points.

■ Successful *wall play* with a *third man* is worth two bonus points.

Coaching:

- Visual perception should not only be deep but also wide. Use entire 180-degree angle of vision (*passing intelligence*).
- Wall players can also play the *high wall pass* (*passing tactics*).
- All players should risk playing faulty *wall passes* (*passing mindset*).

Variations:

- Add two neutral players next to each of the two goals to ramp up the deep ball.
- Mark the playing field longer and narrower.
- Speed-wall passing: only 8 sec to the finish.

4.3.13 THE ANGLED PASS

"The elementary steps that define a good player are that he receives the ball, passes."

(Angel Cappa—Argentine coach)

During an international game against the US, the German goalie Marc-André ter Stegen, with the ball at his foot in his own penalty box, had the agonizing choice of either hitting a long ball forward to bridge the blocked space in the center or passing to the left back who at this moment was nearly parallel to the goalie near the touchline and could still be passed to.

The result is well known. The left back passed back to ter Stegen who couldn't control the ball, leading to an own goal.

For the purpose of practice and instruction, all passes, short or long, should have a specific angle: *angled pass*, not *square*, as the following practice example illustrates. The opponent can reach *square passes* more quickly. This makes the parallel position of the two central defenders in a *back four* or double six in a 1-4-3-3 (point to the front) to each other particularly difficult for continued effective play.

If the *pass* is tied to gaining space, the players without the ball play a central role.

- *Break away* from the opponent. Example: Opponent is close to the offensive player, so either push off from the opponent and immediately sprint toward him or in another direction, or pull clear.
- Get out of the *cover shadow* in the passing gaps (break away in the gaps). Example: Offering a cover gap in which the players can then dribble after passing and receiving the ball.
- Offer support facing the game (*open position*) to be able to immediately pass offensively or dribble towards the opponent. The open position is very important especially at the sides of the field, on the wings, and during buildup. Motto: "In behind into touch!"
- If the ball is not in play, *pre- and post-actions* are critical requirements for effective *passing at an angle*:
    - Starting motions into open space are typical *pre-actions*.
    - Running after one's own pass or moving to a new space is a typical *post-action*.
- *Create passing stations*: left, right, gap, and *advantageous* angles for passing in a rectangular space.

If the teammates without the ball behave appropriately for the situation, the angled pass is an excellent means for gaining space simply and effectively because it can only be defended with effort by the entire opposing team. Moreover, practicing and teaching the *angled pass* is linked with perceiving and practicing the long pass.

The following fig. 102 shows the simulated situation of an *angled pass* by Atletico Bilbao (white/blue) in the center of the field.

The 9er standing off-center (white/blue) moved out of the central defender's cover shadow (see first passing arrow) and stands in the gap for the *angled pass*. This is also the case with the 6er (white/blue) (see second passing arrow). This results in additional passing angles (see third passing arrow) that won't be further elaborated on here. This scene originates from the Atletico Bilbao (white/blue) vs. Atletico Madrid (red/white) European League final on May 5, 2012, at a 0:0 score (action sequence with times: 04:05 to 04:08—ball on the wing—playing time).

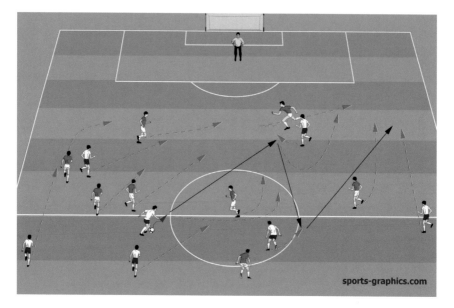

Fig. 102: The angled pass in the 2012 European League final between Atletico Bilbao and Atletico Madrid.

The illustration shows that approximately 50 m of the width of the field can be bridged in approximately 3 sec on the premise of *gaining space* with *angled passes*.

EXAMPLES FOR PRACTICE AND INSTRUCTION

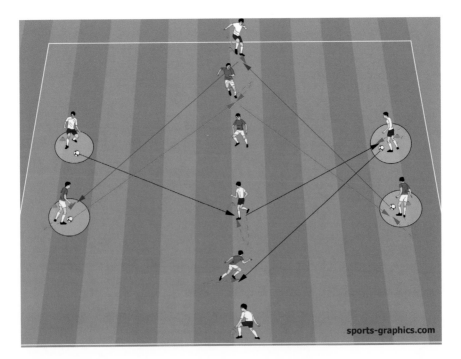

Fig. 103: Grid of 3:3:3

Organization:

- Set up three cones vertically and horizontally in each of three rows and lines. Distances are based on skill level and intent.
- One player at each cone, 10 players total.
- The outside players in the two middle rows are in possession (four players and four balls).

Progression:

- Balls can only be passed at a *specific angle* and are continuously on the move.
- Coach or instructor and players determine the passing angles together.

Coaching:

- Occasionally tie up/stop a ball when there is too much passing chaos (*passing tactics*).

- "Chin up and look around!" (180-degree movement perception; *passing intelligence*)
- Quick and incisive passes back to the partner.

Variations:

- Passing with two balls.
- Passing with one ball.
- Execute a *body feint* after each pass (see Hyballa and te Poel 2013).

Fig. 104: 8v8 at three large goals with goalies

Organization:

- 8v8 at three large goals with goalies on one half of a playing field.

Progression:

- Open play.
- Play only *angled passes*.
- As soon as a straight pass is played the opposing team gets a penalty kick.
- One team plays at both large goals and must immediately look for the finish.
- The opposing team plays at the large goal and can operate unrestricted.

Coaching:

- "First go deep, then go wide!" (*Passing technique*)

- The players without the ball are constantly moving and trying to get out of the cover shadow (*passing fitness*).
- The 6er and 10er should frequently be positioned behind the opponent so that he isn't immediately aware of their running paths (out of the cover shadow) (Motto: "Hide and then suddenly come out of the shadow!" (*Passing intelligence*)

Variations:

- Play with only one to two touches.
- The team that plays at the two large goals must finish after 8 sec.
- Always play forward (*passing mindset*).

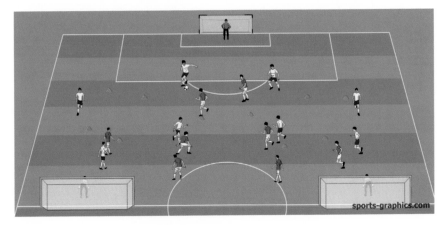

Fig. 105: 8v8 at three large goals with angle cone goals

Organization: See figure 104.

Progression:

- See figure 104 in which the passes on the field must always be played through various cone goals.

Coaching:

- Players should approach with a fast dribble before passing (*passing technique*).
- The player without the ball must look for a connection with the passing player (active coaching: hand signals, code words) (*passing intelligence*).
- Players must try to resolve situations with short passes (*passing philosophy*).

Variations:

- Open play.

- Rule: The team that situationally does not want to play at the cone goals must finish after 6 sec.

- Always play forward (*passing mindset*).

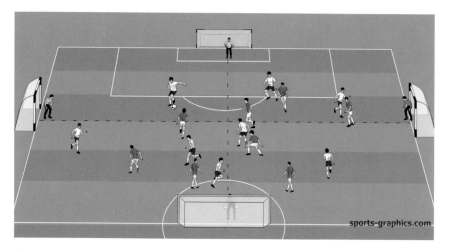

Fig. 106: 8v8 in four zones at four large goals with four goalies

Organization:

- 8v8 at four large goals with goalies on one half of a playing field.

- The playing field is divided into four zones with a vertical and a horizontal line. Mark with cones or colored marking tape.

Progression:

- Open play.

- Passes must be played *vertically* or *diagonally*.

- *Square passes* are not allowed.

Coaching:

- Long switch passes are also an option (*passing tactics*)

- Ball should be played incisively into the running path (*passing technique*).

- No hasty passes into open space (*passing mindset*).

Variations:

- "Caution! Changing playing conditions!" Each zone now has different touch limits (high degree of difficulty).
- Ask for *ground passes*.

11V11—NO SQUARE PASSES!

Organization:

- 11v11 on a large playing field.

Progression:

- Open play, but *square passes* are not allowed.
- If a *square pass* is played, the opposing team gets a penalty kick.

Coaching:

- "Always look forward!"
- The ball is played vertically to the rear or the front.
- Players without the ball create situations for *angled passes* (*passing tactics*).

Variations:

- Play on a three-quarter field.
- Play on one half of a field.
- If a *square pass* is played, the player must immediately dribble and offensively provoke a 1v1.

4.3.14 THE HEAD PASS

"Practice doesn't make perfect, perfect practice makes perfect."

(Franz Beckenbauer)

The following two situations often occur during competitive play:

1. An attacker is positioned at the *back post* during a set piece and heads the ball to a teammate.
2. The goalie deflects the ball from the ground, and the midfielder in a 1v1 heads it directly in front of the 10er's feet as an assist.

Most often these two example game situations develop into well-thought out *attacking* and *finishing actions*.

As described, the header is considered a head pass. It is, of course, different from a pure offensive or defensive header. Accordingly, the *head pass* does *not* aim to score a direct goal or to prevent a goal.

It goes without saying that the *head pass* must be learned and practiced during training and instruction.

The following fig. 107 shows the simulated situations of a purposeful head pass by the 6er of Ajax Amsterdam (white/blue) to the left wingback (white/blue) in a common 1v1 situation in the center of the field. Seven other controlled and well-thought out passing and dribbling actions developed from this and eventually led to a 2-0 win against NEC Nijmegen. The scene stems from the March 31, 2013, game between Ajax Amsterdam (white/blue) and NEC Nijmegen (red/white) in the Dutch soccer league, at a 1-0 score (action sequence with times: 76:08 to 76:27 minutes of playing time).

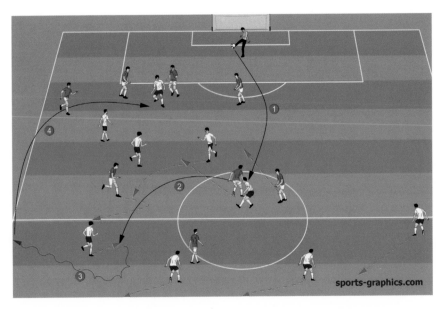

Fig. 107: The head pass in the game Ajax Amsterdam vs. NEC Nijmegen in the Dutch soccer league

The illustration shows the purposeful *head pass* to the rear in the direction of the left defender who opens up, turns, dribbles, and then plays a chip pass on the wing to the 9er, who triggers additional automatisms until the finish. This is also supported by the approximately 19 sec of playing time (relatively long) until the finish.

EXAMPLES FOR PRACTICE AND INSTRUCTION

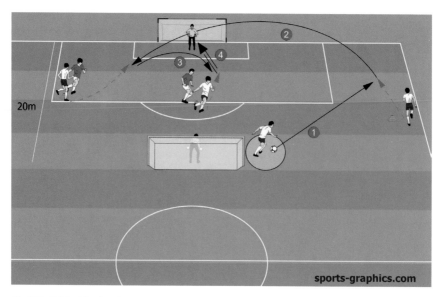

Fig. 108: Finish with a head pass and changeover at two goals

Organization:

- Two large goals (with goalies) are set up approximately 20 m apart.

Progression:

- Two *head pass players* can be chosen who must head the ball to their respective center forward.

- When two players attack, two players should immediately play as opposing defensive players (*2v2 situations plus goalie in the penalty box*).

- If the finish is unsuccessful immediately play at the other goal, the changeover.

Coaching:

- Play the *head pass* incisively even with an opponent (*passing mindset*).

- *Do not play the head pass square* but rather angled (*passing tactics*).

- Ask for immediate changeover from offense to defense and vice versa (*passing philosophy*). The goalie always actively participates in the game.

Variations:

■ Head the ball directly to the goalie and then play 2v2.

■ Play a direct *head pass* at goal.

■ Play a *head pass* to the goalie and then immediately look for the 1v1 with the opposing player.

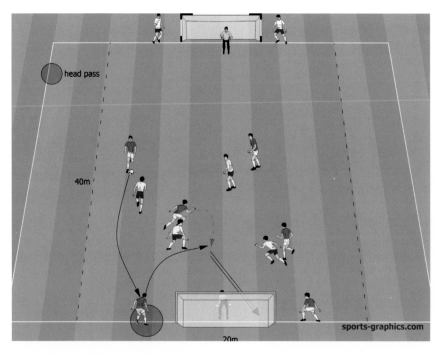

Fig. 109: 4v4 plus 4 head pass assistants

Organization:

■ 4v4 at two large goals with goalies on a playing field that is 40 x 20 m.

■ Two neutral players are positioned next to each large goal.

Progression:

■ Open play.

■ Two neutral players are positioned next to each of the two large goals and after a head pass must head the ball back onto the field (head ball assist).

Coaching:

- The *volley* must be played hard and incisive (*passing technique*).

- Also look for the *third player* when playing a *head pass* (*passing tactics*).

- When playing the *head pass*, aim for the centers' feet. Objective: To make receiving the ball easy (*passing technique and tactics*).

Variations:

- The *head pass* can only be played to the player who passed the ball.

- The *head pass* must be played to the *third player*.

- A goal after a *head pass* counts as double. But the neutral players can now also receive *ground passes* (*passing intelligence*).

Fig. 110: 4v4 plus 4 head pass players on the wings

Organization: See fig. 109.

Progression:

- The *head pass* players now play on the wing (sides of field).

Coaching:

- Play *incisive chip* balls to the wingers.
- Play *head passes* forcefully into the center (*passing mindset*).
- Also play the *head pass* to the back post (*passing intelligence*).

Variations:

- Mark a zone in front of the goal that the ball must be headed into (*passing technique*).
- On the field the ball is headed only, and only the neutral players on the wing can now also use *foot passing techniques*.
- All players, including the goalie, can only play head passes (*passing technique*).

11V11 IN ONE HALF OF THE FIELD WITH HEAD PASSES

Organization:

- 11v11 at two large goals with goalie on one half of the field.

Progression:

- Open play.
- Goals can only be scored if a *head pass* was played as an assist.

Coaching:

- In addition to combinations, alternately play a quick switch pass to the teammate's head (*passing intelligence*).
- "Push the head pass into the center or to the back post!" (*Passing technique and mindset*)
- Also pass to the *back of a teammate's head* in order to surprise the opponent with a flick on to the own 9er (*passing intelligence or creativity*).

Variations:

- All players play with their heads.
- Goal must be scored with a header.
- Assist and finish (both) must be done with a header.

4.3.15 THE THROW-IN PASS

"If you want to become a champion you must play against champions."

(Svetislav Pesic, Bayern Munich basketball coach, in the Frankfurter Allgemeine Zeitung, January 17, 2014, No. 14, pg. 28)

Because the *throw-in pass* is the only pass played by hand by a field player, it generally does not get much attention in soccer practice. A common perception is: "Anyone can do a throw-in! Both feet on the ground and hands and ball behind the head, and there you go."

However, it is still important to address some technical and tactical details that coaches and instructors should not miss and that speak for the relevant training of the *throw-in pass.*

- The player making the throw-in is in possession (*passing philosophy*).
- During a throw-in pass the opponent *on the field has a superior number*, which seems trivial at this point, and the team in possession is *outnumbered*. Many players are not *aware* of these facts at that moment.
- Is the opponent organized or disorganized? The timing of the throw-in depends on this decision, to throw in quickly or slowly (*passing tactics*).
- *Throw-in passes* must be incisive (*passing technique*).
- Nearly every *throw-in pass* is a waist-high ball for the teammates so that it first must be received with technical precision (*receiving technique*).
- Moreover long *throw-in passes*, particularly into the opposing danger zone can be an effective means for generating scoring opportunities near the goal (see UEFA 2012a, pg. 10)

The following fig. 111 shows the simulated situation of a *throw-in pass* by Alves (FC Barcelona) (red/white) to his teammate Messi (red/white) on their own right wing in their half. Messi makes a *direct volley pass* (receiving the ball) at a run toward the player making the throw-in and is thus *double teamed* by two players from Manchester United (white/blue).

After the *volley back-pass* to Alves the FC Barcelona's 6er, Busquets, moves up toward the same and thereby forms a *passing triangle* in a 4v4 near the player making the throw-in. Alves plays a *give-and-go pass* with Messi who lets the ball rebound to the 6er, who is moving up because the second Manchester United player has shifted from Messi toward Alves. This suspended the *double-teaming* on the wing. Messi sees that his 1v2 has become a 1v1, and after his *triangle pass* to Busquets, he runs at top speed behind his opponent who is still moving forward. Busquets plays a *flat pass* into Messi's path, who gets behind Manchester's *back four* into the *open space* to the goal.

This scene is from the FC Barcelona (red/white) vs. Manchester United (white/blue) Champions League final in May, 2011, at a 0-0 score (action sequence with times: 08:46 to 08:52 minutes—ball is back with the 10er—of playing time).

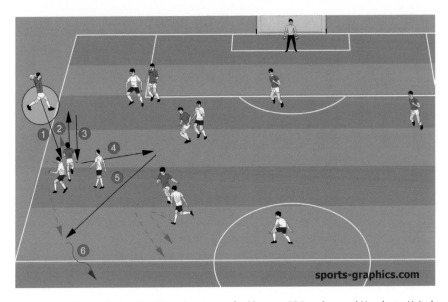

Fig. 111: Throw-in pass in the 2011 Champions League final between FC Barcelona and Manchester United

The illustration shows the great importance of receiving the ball after a *throw-in pass* and the previously mentioned tactical implications after the player making the throw-in gets back on the field.

EXAMPLES FOR PRACTICE AND INSTRUCTION

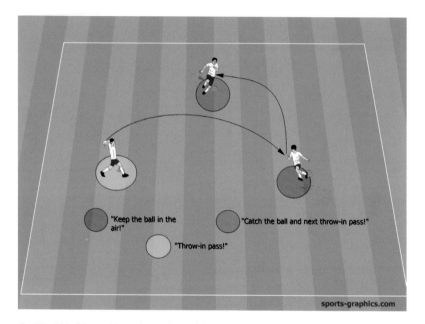

Fig. 112: Grid of three with starting action and throw-in pass

Organization:

■ Three players stand facing each other.

■ They practice with one ball.

■ Change distances based on skill level and training goals.

Progression:

■ The player in the circle holds the ball in his hands and begins to execute the throw-in pass, throwing alternately to one or the other teammate.

■ The player receiving the ball must first *keep the ball in the air* and then play it to the next player.

■ This player then executes another throw-in.

Coaching:

- Make some throws to the head and some throws to the feet (*passing technique*).

- "Put some power behind that ball!" (*Passing mindset* for a long ball)

Variations:

- The *throw-in pass* is directed at the head.

- The *throw-in pass* should only be directed at the feet.

- Add one large goal with goalie to practice the finish (*passing mindset*).

Fig. 113: Grid of five with quick throw-in passes

Organization:

- Four players form a *diamond* on the playing field.

- One player stands in the center of the *diamond*.

- Change distances based on training goals.

- Use one ball.

Progression:

- The player in the circle throws the ball to the teammate in the center.
- The coach or instructor directs: "*Rebound* the ball, play with the right foot, pass to [a specific player]!"
- After several actions, change positions.

Coaching:

- Throw in even if the central player isn't ready (element of surprise).
- "Throw in without much spin!" (*Passing technique*)
- Throw in from a short distance with lots of precision (*passing mindset*).

Variations:

- The four players forming the *diamond* all hold a ball. The central player decides who will pass him the ball.
- The central player executes 10 quick *throw-in passes*, and the four players in the diamond must react with situational ball control (*passing technique*).
- The central player plays a no-look pass to the next player in the diamond, who must react immediately.

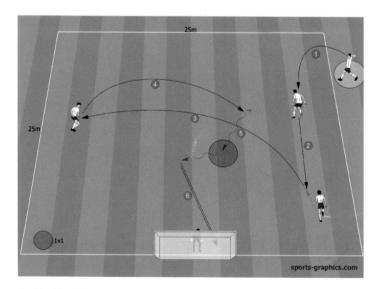

Fig. 114: Throw-in passes with switch pass and finish

Organization:

- Four players play at a large goal with goalie on a playing field that is 25 x 25 m.

Progression:

- The player in the circle throws the ball to the teammate who flicks the *throw-in pass* on another player with his head or foot.
- The player plays a direct *switch pass* to the fourth teammate.
- This player catches the ball and immediately throws it to the second player (attacker) who must play a 1v1 against the *switch pass player* (defender) who is moving in.

Coaching:

- Play quick sequences and progressions (*passing fitness*).
- Short *throw-in pass* equals extreme precision, long *throw-in pass* equals power (speed) (*passing tactics and intelligence*).
- The player making the throw-in can also *throw the ball into space* to prompt the player without the ball to actively gain space (*passing mindset and philosophy*).

Variations:

- Players do not play a 1v1, but rather play at the goal together as two forwards.
- The attacker does not have to shoot directly at the goal because he gets the option of *shifting* to a player making the throw-in (*passing intelligence*).
- The player in the circle plays a short throw-in pass to his teammate, who lets the ball *rebound*, followed by a long *throw-in pass* to the other teammate, who must finish.

Fig. 115: 4v4 plus 4 throw-in pass players

Organization:

- 4v4 plus 4 on a 40-x-25-m playing field at two large goals with goalies.

Progression:

- Open play.
- The four neutral players standing at the sidelines can only make throw-ins.
- A goal scored after a *throw-in* counts double.

Coaching:

- "*Chip* the ball to the player making the throw-in!" (*Passing technique*)
- Once the ball has been played to the outside, the player immediately executes a *post-action* and offers his support (*passing fitness*).
- "Throw the ball to the foot or the head!"

Variations:

- The player making the throw-in must wait 3 sec. before throwing the ball (*passing fitness*).
- If the pass to the player throwing the ball is flat he can also play the ball with his foot (*passing intelligence*).
- The player throwing the ball can also throw it in the goal (*passing mindset*).

Fig. 116: 7v7 with surprise throw-in passes

Organization:

- 7v7 at two large goals with goalies on one half of a playing field.
- Place a number of additional replacement balls at the two sidelines.

Progression:

- Open play.
- During ongoing open play, the coach repeatedly calls for a *throw-in pass*.
- Then a *player near the ball* must sprint toward the sidelines and execute the *throw-in pass*.
- The first ball is a timed pass toward a sideline and then is available again for a *throw-in pass*.

Coaching:

- The player throwing the ball must identify the team's tactical situation and choose the most effective way of executing the *throw-in pass* (*passing intelligence and tactics*).

- Motto: "During a *changeover* the long *throw-in* pass can be most effective!" (*Passing tactics*)

- Motto: "When the opponent is organized, the short (and incisive) *throw-in pass* is the best choice for keeping possession!" (*Passing tactics*)

Variations:

- Short *throw-in passes* only.

- Long *throw-in passes* only.

- If the ball is out, a *throw-in pass* follows (*passing fitness*).

Fig. 117: 8v8 plus 2 with tactical throw-in pass (strategy)

Organization:

- 8v8 at two large goals with goalies on a 60-x-30-m playing field.
- One neutral player is positioned at each of the two sidelines.
- Have lots of replacement balls on hand.

Progression:

- As soon as a ball goes behind the goal line or in touch, a neutral player immediately makes a *throw-in pass* from the wing position.
- The player at the right sideline can only throw short, and the other player can only throw long.
- The teams must react to these two versions.

Coaching:

- "Always keep moving and react to the ball!" (*Passing fitness*)
- "During long *throw-in passes* be prepared for the air duel (1v1) by working on body tension and mindset!" (*Passing mindset and fitness*)
- "During short *throw-in passes* be prepared for the following passing combination: *gap, passing angle, cover shadow, between the lines.*" (*Passing mindset and fitness*)

Variations:

- 9v9 without neutral players (*passing tactics*).
- A goal scored after a *throw-in pass* counts as five points (*passing philosophy*).
- If a throw-in pass results in a turnover, the opponent immediately gets a penalty kick (*passing mindset*).

4.3.16 PASSING INTO SPACE

"How often do you see a pass of more than 40 meters when 20 meters is enough? Or a one-two in the penalty area when there are seven people around you when a simple wide pass around the seven would be the solution?"

(Johan Cruijff, 2007)

Everyone is familiar with a situation that often occurs during practice or a competition: The ball is played into a certain space and no teammate takes up the offer, so the ball goes to the opponent without a fight. The spectators whistle and incomprehension and uncertainty can spread through the team.

Many players are not ready or prepared for a pass into open space without prior verbal or non-verbal communication with the recipient—or an automated and unimpeded combination.

But the *pass into open space* can be an essential element of a *creative tactical action*:

- The players do not always pass the ball to a specific recipient (*element of surprise*).
- The pass into a certain space must be played courageously (*willingness to take risks*).
- The teammate without the ball is prompted to run into space (*stimulative nature*).

- In today's soccer, passes into the seams, vertical passes, and *up-and-over passes* into spaces are considered *essential characteristics of highly creative and successful players* (see Memmert 2013d).

- The pass is played purposefully into a space in which the opposing team is already located. The opponent takes possession and is immediately put under pressure in the space by the other team's counterattack (see chapter 4.5). Pep Guardiola says the following: "When you attack with the ball the opponent is in defensive formation. Give him the ball, and they all run forward. When you then take the ball away from the opponent, by the time they have all turned around you are right in front of their goal. But you have to be very tight to get the ball right back after the turnover" (quote from Schulze-Marmeling 2013, pg. 185).

- In some game situations the player on the ball can be perplexed and helpless. At such a point a *pass into space* can help him solve his problem *independently*, even if at first glance this method appears to be ineffective (Schulze-Marmeling 2013, pg. 185).

The following fig. 118 shows the simulated situation of a (*one-touch*) *pass into space* by Ribéry (FC Bayern Munich) (red/white) to his teammate Müller (red/white). Kroos initiates this combination from the center of the field with a *switch pass* played with the outside of the foot to Ribéry in the opposing half. He is in a position on the left wing and plays a long *pass into space with one touch* into the seam between wingback and central defender (white/blue). After a *pre-action*, Müller sprints (in an arc) between the two central defenders (white/blue) into this *pass into the seam*.

This scene stems from the Champions League game on Oct. 2, 2013, between Manchester City (white/blue) and FC Bayern Munich (red/white) at a 0-0 score (action sequence with times: 08:46 to 08:52 minutes—ball in space behind back four— of playing time.

Fig. 118: Passing into space in the Champions League game between Manchester City and FC Bayern Munich

The illustration emphasizes the above preliminary remarks about creative tactical actions via *passes into space*.

EXAMPLES FOR PRACTICE AND INSTRUCTION

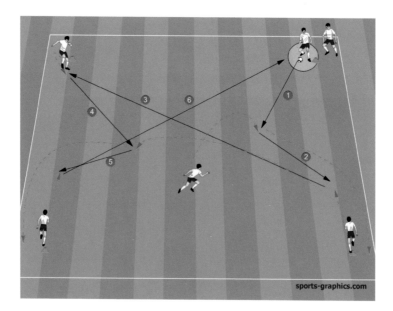

Fig. 119: Ball into space—run into space

Organization:

- A grid of four (with four cones and eight players) and several balls.
- Distances based on skill level and training goal (*short or long passes into space*).

Progression:

- The player in the circle passes the ball diagonally into space.
- The player diagonally opposite him tries to chase down the ball. He starts only after the ball has been played. The *pass into space* is timed so that the player can reach it in time.
- The player lets the ball *rebound* into the short, open space to the player opposite him, who plays a *long pass into space* to the player in the back.
- Both players switch positions and thereby carry out pre- and post-actions.
- The passing combination is then smoothly transitioned and continued on the other side.

Coaching:

- The player must react quickly to the ball (*passing fitness*).
- The players must keep a constant eye on their spaces (*passing intelligence*).
- "Follow the ball with your eyes!"

Variations:

- Increase distances.
- Frequently play a *wall pass* to the teammate's foot (*passing intelligence*).
- Set up a second grid of four via mirroring. The grids of four can be left or switched with a *switch pass* in the sense of shifting play (*passing tactics*).

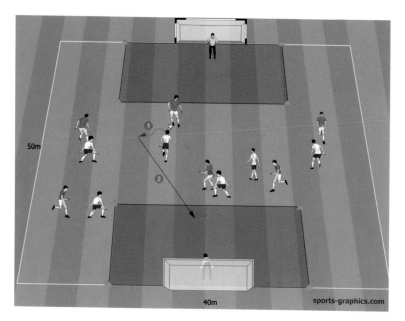

Fig. 120: Variation: Accompanying the ball

Organization:

- 6v6 at two large goals with goalies on a playing field that is 50 x 40 m.
- A zone 20 m wide is marked off with cones in the center of the field.

Progression:

- The players can sprint into the *end zones* (dark areas) only after the ball has been played (*passing tactics*).
- The teammate on the ball forces the player without the ball to start into space (*passing mindset*).
- The defenders also cannot run into the end zones before the *pass into space* has been played.

Coaching:

- Ask for lots of *flat passes* through the seams (*passing intelligence*).
- The ball should be played in such a way that it can be accompanied.
- When the opponent receives the ball, the team immediately switches to a counter press. Motto: "We can score even when the opponent has the ball!" (*Passing tactics*)

Variations:

- Increase or decrease field measurements.

- 7v5: The outnumbered team can also pass the ball to the foot. This is meant to tempt (i.e., challenge) the superior numbers team into pressing (*passing philosophy*).

- After accompanying the ball, either a shot at goal must be taken or a 1v1 must be sought (*passing mindset*).

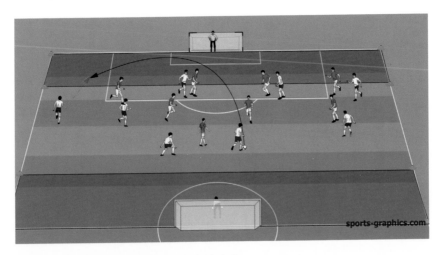

Fig. 121: Variation: Accompanying the ball with chip balls

Organization:

- 8v8 at two large goals with goalies on one half of a large playing field.

Progression:

- See fig. 120 in which the balls must now be chipped (*passing technique*).

- Keep looking for the wings, especially when all the opposing players' efforts are ball-oriented, and they are focusing on the ball (*passing philosophy and intelligence*).

Coaching:

- The ball must be chipped from the center of the middle zone.

- Choose an alternative: Play a *switch pass* into open space (*passing intelligence*).

- "Rule: Start running after the ball has been played because the attacker always has the advantage!" (*Passing tactics and philosophy*)

Variations:

- The players can hold the ball in their hands and play it into space as a *volley pass* (*surprise element*).
- Play on three-quarters of a large field to initiate *longer passes into space* (*passing technique*).
- The player without a ball decides when the ball is passed into space. The chief without a ball blasts off into a certain space and receives the ball there (*passing technique and philosophy*).

Fig. 122: Passes into space behind the goals

Organization:

- 8v8 at two large goals with goalies between the centerline and penalty area.
- Mark off a zone 10 m *deep* behind the two large goals.
- Decrease the width of the field to the width of the penalty area.

Progression:

- Open play in which goals can also be scored.
- Additional option: The ball can be *passed* or *chipped* behind the goal, and the attacker can pass the ball into the field with a *back pass* with the intent of scoring a subsequent goal.

Coaching:

- "Pay attention to timing of the *pass into space!*" (*Passing technique and tactics*)
- Forward must react quickly (*passing fitness*).
- Accompany the *pass into space* (*passing tactics*)

Variations:

- If the attacker reaches the ball before the defender does, the attacker gets a bonus point (*passing mindset*).
- If the ball is played into the back zone all players must move across a *centerline to be marked off* in order to immediately execute a counter-press with a tight net in the event of a turnover (*passing philosophy and mindset*).
- If a goal is scored with a header after an assist or a *second to last ball* from the back zone, it counts as triple (*passing intelligence*).

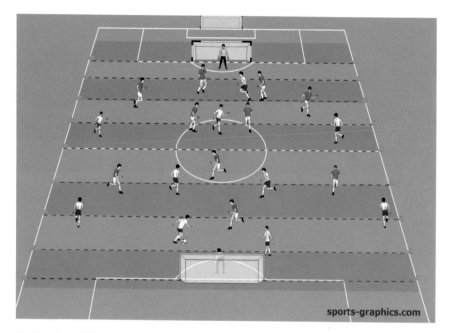

Fig. 123: The ball blasts into the zone, and then the player blasts into the zone!

Organization:

- 11v11 from penalty area to penalty area at two large goals with goalies.
- Divide and mark off the playing field into eight *lateral zones.*

Progression:

- The ball can only be played for 4 to 6 sec (depending on skill and training level) in one zone.
- The ball must quickly alternate between *width* and *depth.*
- In doing so the player on the ball is the chief on the ball.

Coaching:

- Ask for deep *flat passes* (*passing tactics*).
- Practice *chip balls* on the wings.
- "Chief on the ball! Decide to make your *pass into space* in good time!" (*Passing mindset*)

Variations:

- Decrease the size of the playing field and ask for *flat passes* only (*passing technique*).

- The ball can bridge the space between the *defensive* and *offensive zone* only with a *long pass*.

- Mark an end zone in front of the opposing goal and frequently pass the ball into this space (*promoting willingness to take risks*). If the attacker is in possession he can play the 1v1 against the goalie by himself (*passing mindset and fitness*).

4.3.17 THE ONE-TOUCH PASS

"When we are at our maximum and we're playing our quick passing game, it's outstanding. It's one-touch football and it destroys the opposition. Today in training we played four against four and everyone touched the ball in six seconds. One touch, one pass, cut it back and score."

(Robin van Persie, formerly of FC Arsenal London, presently Manchester United)

In today's soccer everyone talks about *one-touch passing*: playing with just one touch of the ball.

Often the ball is passed from one teammate to the next this way. Ostensibly and seen strictly from the mastery of *passing techniques* point of view, it is an easily trained movement characteristic. But seen in a game-situational context, the following characteristics must be taken into account in practice and instruction:

- The pre-actions that are essentially responsible for the success of a situational *one-touch pass* (*open and closed position relative to the ball*).
- The option of passing to the third man.
- Letting the ball *rebound* to the passing player.
- Can the player *open* the game with one touch or does the *one-touch pass* contribute to purposive *possession*?
- If the field is very small (tight), it is important to be able to break away. At such a time a *one-touch pass* would be a time and stress regulator because it would help, for instance, to promptly shift to another space without losing possession.

The following fig. 124 shows the simulated situation of a *one-touch pass into the seam* by an Atletico Madrid midfielder (white/blue) from a half-open position (after a previous *give-and-go pass* with the left central defender and subsequent pre-action) to the left winger running into space. This player crosses the ball *in behind the defense* and to the advancing 9er.

The scene is from the European League final on May 9, 2012, between Atletico Bilbao (red/white) and Atletico Madrid (white/blue) at a 0-0-score (action sequence with times: 01:36 to 01:42 minutes—cross to the 9er near the goal—of play).

Fig. 124: The one-touch pass in the 2012 European League final between Atletico Bilbao and Atletico Madrid

The illustration exemplarily shows several characteristics outlined at the beginning: The outnumbered 2v3 situation (for the attacker on the wing; small field) until the cross can be resolved effectively with a long (dosed) and quick *one-touch pass* within 6 sec.

EXAMPLES FOR TRAINING AND PRACTICE

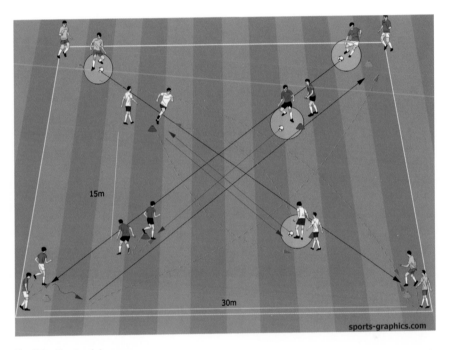

Fig. 125a: One-touch in squares

Organization:

- In a 30-x-30-m square, mark off an additional 15-x-15-m square.
- Each square is manned with eight players (two players at each cone).
- The players facing each other form a group: red with red, blue with blue, etc. Each group has a ball.

Progression:

- In both squares, players pass each other the ball diagonally and flat. One-touch is mandatory in the inner square.

- The passing players chase after their ball.
- If the position changes get too hectic, the players in the outer square can, if needed, receive and control the balls to the side and only then pass.
- The players in the inner circle switch with those in the outer circle as specified by the coach or instructor (time limits depending on training goal and skill level).

Coaching:

- "Keep your eyes open and always keep moving!" (*Passing fitness*)
- Coach each other with designated code words (*passing philosophy*).
- Time the passes and running paths; put feeling into the ball because there are up to three opposing balls in play (*passing technique and mindset*).

Variations:

- Allow one to two touches. Pay attention to situational context (*passing intelligence*).
- Ask for both feet to be used (*passing technique*).
- Add different types of balls (large or small, heavy or light) (*passing technique*).
- Add mini goals and have lots of replacement balls on hand.

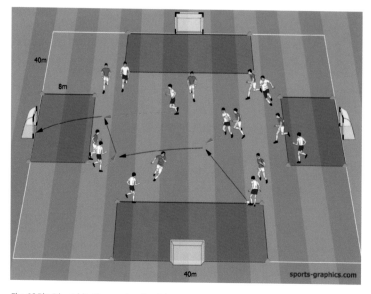

Fig. 125b: Direct hit—The one-touch mini game

Organization:

- 8v8 in a 40-x-40-m square.
- A mini goal is set up on each of the square's sidelines.
- An 8-m taboo zone is marked off in front of each mini goal.

Progression:

- *One-touch passes.*
- Each team defends two diagonally adjacent goals.
- Goals must be scored direct from outside the zones.

Coaching:

- Incisive passing (*passing technique*).
- Precept: The passing player always becomes the pass recipient (*passing fitness*).
- "Courage for the risky touch!" (*Passing mindset*).

Variations:

- Mark mini goals with colored bibs or cones and change the direction of play at the coach's or instructor's command ("Team red to yellow!") (*Passing intelligence*).

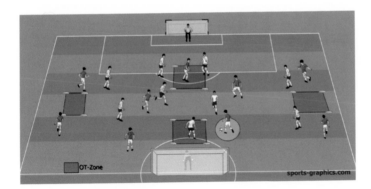

Fig. 126: 9v9 with one-touch zones

Organization:

- 9v9 on one half of a field at two large goals with goalies.
- A total of four 7-x-7-m *one-touch zones* are marked off on this field, and the two central zones are called *offensive zones.*

Progression:

- Open play in a specific tactical formation.
- If the ball is played into a *one-touch zone*, it can only be played with one touch in this zone as well.
- The defending team cannot attack in the *one-touch zone*.

Coaching:

- During *buildup* choose a confident and incisive passing game out of the *one-touch zone* (*passing technique*).
- Fire and risk-taking in the offensive one-touch zones (*passing mindset*).
- The passing player immediately becomes the pass receiver (*passing fitness*).

Variations:

- Decrease or increase the size of *one-touch zones*.
- *One-touch* only in the center: 8v8 at two large goals with goalies on two-thirds of a large playing field. Mark off a middle zone 25 x 30 m wide from penalty area to penalty area. Direct play is mandatory in the middle zone.
- Coach's darlings: Only two to three players are allowed to play one-touch passes. The coach or instructor picks the players.
- The emotional rollercoaster: 1 minute of open play and 1 minute of one-touch soccer.

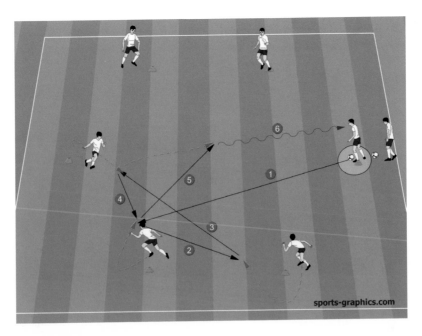

Fig. 127: Grid of six: Buildup with one-touch passes

Organization:

- At least one player is positioned at each cone in a grid of six.
- The position of the player in the circle must be manned multiple times.
- Distances between cones depend on the respective training goal.

Progression:

- The player in the circle dribbles. In a competitive game, he is number 4/5. He plays a diagonal pass (skip a row) to one of the players positioned at the sides, in a competitive game positions 2 and 8 (left side) or positions 3 and 7.
- This player lets the ball *rebound* to the skipped player 2/3.
- The central 6er anticipates this double action early on and readies to receive a pass. He receives the *one-touch pass* from 2/3 and lets it rebound to 7/8.
- The 6er receives the return *wall pass* and does a fast dribble to the starting point of the *one-touch combination*.
- Every passing player moves up one position.
- Switch sides.

Coaching:

- Quick and incisive one-touch passing game (*passing technique*).
- Pass next to the body in the direction of the outside foot (also for the purpose of controlling the ball).
- Execute running feints.
- Control the ball from an *open position.*
- Change pace and direction (*passing fitness*).
- Keep up intensive communication—verbal and non-verbal (*passing mindset*).

Variations:

- Simultaneous combinations to both sides (increase number of players and balls).
- Set up two mini goals next to the starting point for combinations. These must be
   a. played at directly with a penetrating pass after the *wall pass* (use both feet), or
   b. passed at quickly and incisively from a fast dribble.
- Set up a mini goal at the imaginary 10er or 9er position and a *penetrating pass* from the 6er into the mini goal.
- Same setup but use several mini goals in different playing directions (positions 7, 9, 11, and 9/10, etc.)

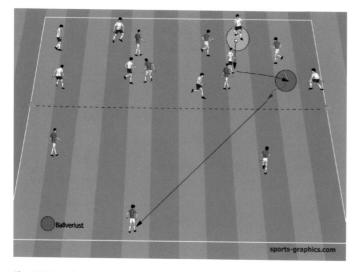

Fig. 128: 8v5 plus 3 in turns—holding on to the ball and changing over to offense with one-touch passes

Organization:

- 8 (white/blue) against 5 (red/white) on a marked off first playing field.
- Three outnumbered players (red/white) position on a second adjoining field of the same size (the angle distorts the two equally large fields).
- Keep one ball and replacement balls handy at the edge of the field.
- Choose field sizes based on skill level and training goal. For example, U19: from the 18-yd box (with external dimensions) to the centerline (first field), and from the centerline to the second 18-yd box (second field).

Progression:

- The superior numbers team plays for possession with *one-touch passes.*
- After gaining possession, the outnumbered team should switch with a pass (*e.g., switch pass*) to the other field with the three teammates as quickly as possible.
- The outnumbered team has open play.
- *Moving up* after switching fields creates a new 8v5.
- Three of the players on the team that lost the ball on the first field remain on their field

Coaching:

- "Stagger yourselves!" The three outnumbered players position on their field so that a *deep ball* can be played when their five teammates on the opposing field gain possession and the trailing players have open space to purposefully *move up* (e.g., circling up and positioning two central players for possession play *with one-touch passes*) (*passing tactics*).
- Ask outnumbered players to actively *block spaces; control the direction of passes; put pressure on the ball* (the player near the ball runs toward the opposing player); *put pressure on the space* (the teammate plays behind the pressing player, blocks the passing lane, and controls the opponent's game); and carry out feigned attacks.
- "Do not run blindly toward the ball! Observe, communicate, take up your defensive positions!"

Variations:

- Decrease or increase the size of the playing fields (*passing fitness*).
- Limit to one to two touches: If a superior numbers player requires two touches for an error-free pass, he can do so. But subsequently his teammate must make do with one touch. Motto: "Avoid a turnover!" (*Passing tactics and intelligence*)

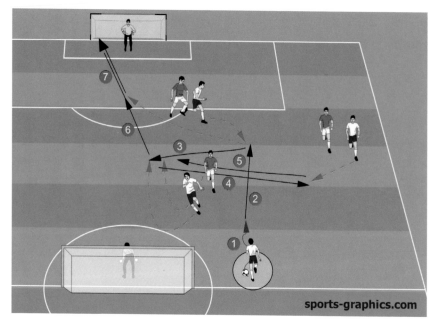

Fig. 129: Tactical group sequences to create scoring opportunities using one-touch passes

Organization:

- 2 x 4 against 3 at one goal with goalie on one-quarter of a large playing field.
- The four players in white/blue and the three players in red/white position themselves as follows:
    a. Blue/white as part of a 1-4-3-3 with forward point or 1-4-2-3-1 (here the 6 has possession, 10, 9 and 7)
    b. Red/white with a central defender, a 2 and a 6
    c. The parallel buildup of the second 4v3 at one goal with goalie is not shown here.

Progression:

- The 6er briefly dribbles; the 10er runs (takes) off to create space.
- The 6er passes to the 9er who is briefly offering support. He lets the ball *rebound* to the 10er who makes a *direct* pass to the wing.
- The 8er immediately plays a *wall pass* back to the 10er who immediately sends the 9er into the lane and the finish.

Coaching:

- Play up-and-over with the first pass to quickly gain space (*passing tactics*).
- Page 263
- The wall pass to the wing is meant to lure the opponent to the outside, creating passing gaps (*passing tactics*).
- The 9er quickly turns, *power*, and goal (*passing tactics and mindset*).

VARIATIONS (TO CREATE SOCRING OPPORTUNITIES)

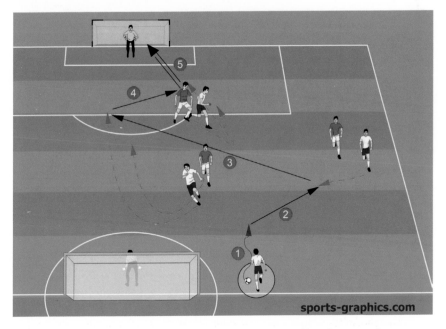

Version B of fig. 129: Tactical group sequences to create scoring opportunities using one-touch passes

- *Version B*: The 6er passes to the winger (7); at the same time the 9er briefly offers his support to the outside to open up the space for the 10er. The 7er immediately plays the ball hard into the path of the 10er who takes it straight to the finish.

- *Version C (without illustration)*: As in Version B, at the end the 10er can play a pass to the 9er *cutting across*. The reason: A second central defender possibly blocks the space for the 9er as part of a tactical team measure or a second forward offers himself for a *wall pass*. Motto: Learn about tactical group solutions.

Version D of fig. 129: Tactical group sequences to create scoring opportunities using one-touch passes

- *Version D*: As in Version B, the 7er sprints after a running feint on the wing, the 10er again opens up the passing lane forward with an *arced run*, and the 6er in possession plays a through ball to the approaching 9er. He lets the ball *rebound* in with one touch to the quickly approaching 7er. If possible this player moves to the inside and plays a quick and incisive pass to the trailing 10er (back post) and 9er (penalty spot) for the finish. Motto: "Don't give the opponent time for organized positional play. A hard, *flat passing game* on the wing is the best option!"

Version E of fig. 129: Tactical group sequences to create scoring opportunities using one-touch passes

■ *Version E*: As before, the 9er lets the ball *rebound* directly into the path of the 10er, who must take a direct shot at goal.

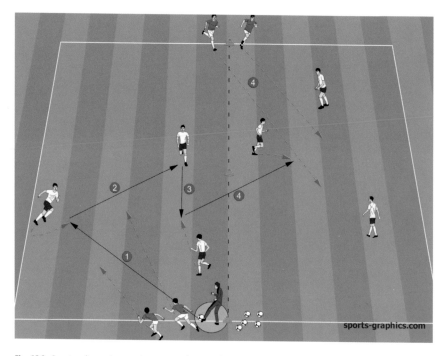

Fig. 130: One-touch passing against aggressive pressing—switch to major pressure from the opponent

Organization:

- 2 x 3 against 2, constantly alternating.
- Two adjoining playing fields.
- Field sizes are based on skill level and training goal.
- Many balls at the edge of the field.
- Playing time is based on skill level and training goal (e.g., Bundesliga: approximately 30 sec. at highest intensity).

Progression:

- Three defenders per playing field and two defenders at the center starting cone.
- The coach or instructor plays a ball onto the respective field at the start and when a ball goes out of play.
- Direct play for the superior numbers team.
- After a minimum of three passes, the superior numbers players can play the ball onto the neighboring field.

- When changing fields, the appropriate players immediately sprint onto the field from the outside and the other pair leaves the field in the direction of the cone.

Coaching (outnumbered team):

- "Keep your head up and constantly be in a ready position." (Passing mindset)
- "Incisive one-touch passing!" (*Passing technique*)
- Get in open positions and choose the triangle as a safe organizational form (*passing tactics*).
- "Keep the space large!" (*Passing tactics*)
- "Make quick decisions!"
- Ask for communication and motivation (*passing mindset*).
- The coach or instructor awards bonus points to players when they absolutely want to keep possession during imprecise passing actions—in other words, facilitate ball salvage actions in the sense of securing and helping (passing mindset).
- "Close to the man? No problem! Play the pass forcefully, and make sure your physical play is fair!" (*Passing mindset*)

Variations:

- Decrease or increase field sizes.
- Increase the number of players.
- Change the playing time.
- Mark off a 2-m corridor between the two fields. The outnumbered team is allowed to play there (making pressing more difficult).
- Back pass only to teammates when the ball relay gets too long (highest level).
- Competitions: See who can keep possession longest, and issue bonus points for every interval and every ball salvage action. Make a chart to keep track of "the one-touch heroes."

4.3.18 TIQUI-TACA SPECIAL—RONDOS

> *"Once again the non-stop combinations originated from field player-goalie Neuer or the central defenders Boateng and Dante, and again did the flat, short precision passes travel to the center via Lahm or to the front via the wingers Rafinha and Alaba, where Kroos or Schweinsteiger or Müller or Ribery or Shaquiri took over with the finest technique at top speed, and with all the assuredness of their soccer skills."*
>
> (Karlheinz Wild in kicker, Oct. 7, 2013, pg.19)

The term *Tiqui-Taca* was coined by the Spanish journalist Andrés Montes who compared the playing style of the Spanish national team in 2006 to *clackers* (in Spanish, *Tiqui-Taca*). Adopted into everyday soccer language, today *Tiqui-Taca* refers to the progression of *Totaalvoetbal* (total football) created by Rinus Michels, Johann Cruijff, Louis van Gaal, and Guus Hiddink (see M. Meijers 2006; Hyballa & te Poel 2013; see chapter 4.4 and 4.5).

Because today's modern soccer is characterized significantly by fitness and dynamics, today's *Tiqui-Taca* might just be the answer: *Positional play* (with constantly changing positions and large running paths) is combined with *possession play* that provides the following important functions with constant attempts to get open, *short passes,* and *triangle passes*:

- To cause the opponent to abandon his *safe, staggered* positional play and fall back on 1v1. This creates open space for the teammates.

- To force the opponent to shift by constantly passing on the ball so that holes opening up in the opponent's ranks can be exploited for the *killer passing game*.

- The team in possession compresses in a certain space, creates superior number situations, and is able to create and quickly man spaces with quick and two-footed *short-pass combination play*, especially in front of the opposing goal.

- The team plays a possession game and patiently waits for an expedient game situation, avoiding rashness, actionism, and high risk (controlling the game). This behavior can be very important for midfield play.

- Sometimes teams use the *short pass game* after very running-intensive game phases (*controlling the space*) as a means for active regeneration. For instance, if the team was able to *quickly* regain possession using counterattacking with a *high line* after a turnover, it is most often followed by dosed *short passes* (and a decrease in the overall playing speed) and resumed planned positions and a safe attack strategy.

At the highest playing level, *Tiqui-Taca* therefore requires an exceptional fitness level and athleticism, above average tactical intelligence and creativity, and unimpeded and variably available *passing techniques*.

The *Rondo* is a form of play that echoes the essential functions of an effective *Tiqui-Taca* as mentioned and can be used to train players in an often fun way. We outline the top ten Rondos with specific focus areas. These have particular connections to the playing philosophies of FC Barcelona under Pep Guardiola and Ajax Amsterdam under Frank de Poer.

The most important technical characteristics of the *Rondos* can be summarized as follows:

- *Short passes* to the foot and into the path
- *Short passes* without spin or rotation
- *Short pass combinations* as a way to take the initiative in competitive play
- "Exude dominance through technical perfection" (see Karlheinz Wild in kicker, Oct. 7, 2013, pg. 19)

- Small-scale *quick pre- and post-actions*
- Two-footed *one-touch combinations*
- Look for holes to pass into (gaps) as a prerequisite for *unimpeded incisive short passes*
- Change initial conditions: *position changes*

We prefer the 8v2/9v3 Rondos in a round or square, or rather rectangular space. When the *Rondo* is played in a square or rectangular form, each player is able to occupy positions that correspond to the team's own formation. If a circular form is chosen the relationship between space and time always remains the same.

An 8v2 *Rondo* gives the players who are trying to get possession the opportunity to test an *agreed upon defensive behavior* (*ball-oriented play, safeguarding each other, offset in depth, situational double-teaming*).

The 9v3 includes elements such as *defensive triangles, hooks, shifting* and makes the *long forward pass* in particular more difficult. The superior numbers in the circle and square or rectangle must learn to adapt to this with *Tiqui-Taca*. In summary it can be said that during a turnover the *Rondo* with its many versions, different time intervals, field sizes, and rules can be an important tool for the planning and implementation of modern soccer practice and instruction.

"Improve your technical and tactical area!"

The following fig. 131 shows the simulated situation with *Tiqui-Taca* in the game between FC Barcelona (red/white) against Real Madrid (white/blue) on Jan. 25, 2012, in the Primera Division. FC Barcelona's 11 passing combinations in Real Madrid's defensive half highlight the great and game-effective importance of *Tiqui-Taca* in the context of the previously mentioned functions: 16 sec. possession with *killer* pass and the subsequent 1-0 FC Barcelona (action sequence with times 34:09 to 34:25 minutes of play).

EXAMPLES FOR PRACTICE AND INSTRUCTION

Fig. 131: Tiqui-Taca in the Primera Division game between FC Barcelona and Real Madrid

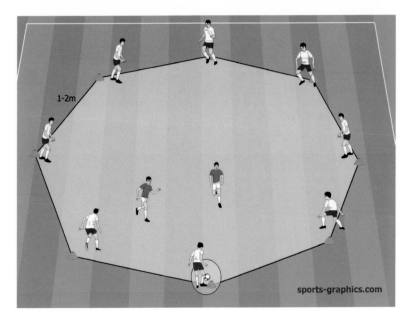

Fig. 132: Rondo 8v2

The distances between players in all of the subsequent Rondos should be determined by group based on skill level and the main focus of training.

Rondo 1 with emphasis on receiving and passing

Progression:
- **Rule 1**: Limit to one to two touches.
- **Rule 2**: Immediately change positions after a turnover, play up to a certain number of turnovers and then switch tasks, or run out the clock.
- **Rule 3**: Switching the playing foot (left, right) is mandatory.
- Alternate rule 3: Use the same playing foot twice.
- Another alternative to rule 3: Three mandatory touches, and the playing foot can be chosen freely.

Coaching:
- Ball control.
- Push pass (*passing technique*).
- Make quick decisions.
- Take the defenders' positions into account.

Rondo 2 with emphasis on push passes over short distances (see fig. 132)

Progression:
- Pass to the player's strong foot.
- See progression, *Rondo 1*

Coaching:
- "Body should be over the ball!"
- "Keep the ball flat!" (*Passing technique*)
- "Stay on the ground and watch your supporting foot because it must be in a game-effective position for the next ball (balance)!"

Rondo 3 with emphasis on ball speed (see fig. 132)

Progression:

- See progression, *Rondo 1*

Coaching:

- "Make the right decision!"
- Choose the ball speed so the defender is spatially and temporally too late (*passing tactics*).

Rondo 4 with emphasis on open space and then the long pass (see fig. 132)

Progression:

- See progression, *Rondo 1*

Coaching:

- Rules for the *long* pass:
    a. Defenders stay in the middle when a *long* pass has been played between two defenders.
    b. Defenders stay in the middle when the ball has been played through the center two to three times.
    c. Defenders stay in the middle when the ball has been passed on for one whole round.
    d. Defenders stay in the middle when the ball has been passed in the Rondo six to eight times without turnover.
    e. Defenders stay in the middle and now practice b and c together (*passing intelligence*).
- Motto: "Lots of space and time for our attacking game!" (*Passing philosophy*)

Rondo 5 with emphasis on the defender waiting (see fig. 132)

Progression:

- See progression, *Rondo 1*

Coaching:

- Short passing game to the other side of the *Rondo* (*passing tactics*).

> **Rondo 6 with emphasis on spatial awareness and directional changes (see fig. 132)**

Progression

- See progression, *Rondo 1*
- Rule: The player in possession cannot play the ball back to the adjacent player.

Coaching:

- Alternate between short and long passes (*passing technique*).
- "Skip a line!"

> **Rondo 7 with emphasis on forms of communication with and without the ball (see fig. 132)**

Progression:

- Use two touches.
- See progression, *Rondo 1*

Coaching:

- "Look around and coach each other!"
- Use the ball speed as a means of communication.
- Pay attention to geometry: Long balls keep the defenders from stepping in because the longer distances require them to run more (*passing tactics*).
- Two touches mean: Control the *Rondo* with the first touch.
- "If you use a hard pass it means: You don't have time!"
- A long pass between two defenders means:

a. To the defender: You have little time.

b. To the attacker: You now have space and time (*passing intelligence*).

- The ball stays in motion, so the defenders cannot rest (*passing fitness*).
- Slow ball as bait: The defender approaches and then a long pass follows (*passing tactics*).

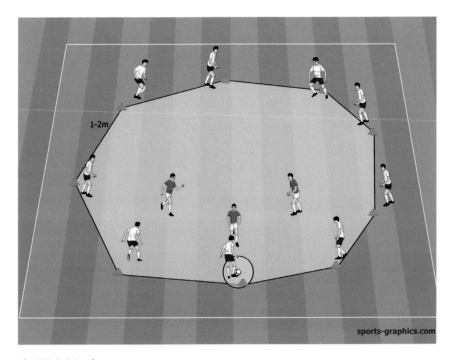

Fig. 133: 9v3 Rondo

Rondo 8 with emphasis on changeover

Progression:

- **Rule 1**: With possession, both or all three outnumbered players must try to get the ball followed by player exchange.
- **Rule 2**: The outnumbered players kick the ball out of play and move up, and the superior numbers players try to immediately win back the ball.
- **Rule 3**: See rule 2 with a marked-off field is set up for the *Rondo* (field size based on skill level). On this field the outnumbered players, when in possession, must

pass the ball incisively and move up. This field must be taken over by the superior numbers players by regaining possession.

- **Rule 4**: If a superior numbers player loses the ball, he immediately becomes a defender. The outnumbered player who won the ball immediately becomes an attacker.
- **Rule 5**: After a turnover the coach or instructor immediately sends a player back into the center. Reason: to keep the game fast.
- **Rule 6**: After a turnover, the coach or instructor quickly passes a new ball into the game.
- **Rule 7**: Whenever the superior number loses the ball, the player who made the bad pass only switches positions with another player from the superior number on the outside (position changes).

Coaching:

- Quick changeover in both directions: Offense to defense and defense to offense (*passing fitness, tactics, and intelligence*).

Rondo 9 with emphasis on passing fitness for Tiqui-Taca

Progression:

- See fig. 133.
- 9v9 with a 1:3 ratio of exertion and recovery.
- One-touch passes in the *Rondo*.

Coaching:

- Outnumbered players with 100% readiness for action.
- Superior numbers players: "Look around and coach each other!"
- See who can make the most passes in a determined amount of time. Competition: "Kings of Rondo" (*Passing mindset*)

Rondo 10 with emphasis on the leader of the game

Progression:

- See fig. 133.
- Players make the rules (see *Rondos* 1-9).

Coaching:

- As a coach or instructor, watch the *Rondo* and give verbal input and let the assistant *ref.*
- Now the players *ref* each other (*passing mindset*).
- One player is named the leader of the game. He carries all the responsibility for the regular flow of the *Rondo*, a fun atmosphere, and his own decisions.

4.3.19 THE FAKE PASS

"Players who are able to con an opponent in 1-on-1 are not only rare, they are precious!"

(Michel Hordijk, athletic director at "Underbouw" and technical coach at Ajax Amsterdam; Münster, 2012)

Today's coach or instructor can find interesting and current training and instruction material on the topic of feints and tricks in soccer from around the world in umpteen videos on YouTube, from professional vendors of soccer videos and DVDs, apps with tracking mode, and video footage from soccer fans. Technique, tricks, and speed are playing an increasingly bigger role in the life of today's youth as well as on the soccer field. Each week Ribéry, Cristiano Ronaldo, Neymar, Robben, Messi, Götze, Reus, Özil, and many others delight the masses when in a game they fake a sideways pass or wrap their foot around the ball and push it off to the other side, followed by a dribble with the outside of the other foot.

A *fake pass* is a part of other *movement combinations* and *body feints*. Some players seem to have boundless *creativity* and *intelligence*; the transitions between individual techniques are fluid, even those of the *fake pass*, which coaches or instructors can read more and more often on the field.

A *fake pass* is a type of deceptive motion indicating a pass that the player does not actually execute. It is like a *passing technique* in its origin. Players often use it to try to get the defenders to change their position relative to the ball in order to get closer to the goal with a pass, shot, or by dribbling.

Often the transitions between techniques cannot be clearly separated, occasionally not even properly characterized, because situations change so quickly. Physical play occurs during tackles, and the tactical creativity of defenders and attackers creates unforeseen events in the course of the game.

The fake pass can therefore usually be seen in three (mixed) forms:

1. The "classic" fake pass, which is most often initiated from a delayed dribble. It is followed by squaring the upper body, like for a *flat pass*, facing forward. The pass is played, but the ball is not touched. Afterward, the ball is often cut back with a quick turning movement, and the player vigorously dribbles away from the opponent into the open space (e.g., Mario Götze, FC Bayern Munich).

2. Video analyses clearly show that after a fake with one foot a *one-touch pass* with the other foot, for example, immediately follows (see the following scene from a game). Combining dribbling and feints and passing are the focus of the game situation.

3. The *shot-at-goal feint* also often originates with a dribble. The player fakes a *shot at goal* with a distinct swinging motion of his dribbling leg and with the position of his upper body and arms (see chapter 4.3.7). This is usually followed by controlling the ball with the outside of the playing foot in the intended direction and the start of a dribble.

The movement dynamics, the change of pace, the timing, the possible alternative actions, and the unimpeded interconnected movements in a game situation or context are the critical parameters for using a *passing feint*. Possible alternative actions are therefore the particular focus of coaching:

- Slow opponent: keep the pace, break through, and finish.
- Fast opponent: Vigorous break-through on the other side against the defender's running path.
- Opponent is too close: Turn *inward or outward* and stand; otherwise carry the ball to the side or diagonally back, then safely open up again.
- If, for instance, the opponent is prompted to move by an oblique dribble he will most likely be forced into a (premature) decision.

In addition, the personality aspect—the player's *Passing Puzzle mindset* during the execution of feints in general—should be particularly emphasized at this time. Feints require a passion for detail, courage, tenacity, self-motivation, goal-orientation, and a sense of responsibility toward the action plan of teammates, coach, and club. The 1v1 situations in particular require playing at top speed while controlling the ball (in the tightest spaces) and thus require the player to have the attitude of wanting to play at the highest risk level, not only from a mental but also from a physical point of view (training management, metering of mental and physical stress).

In practice, this means that mistakes are unavoidable. To get the best from a player presupposes learning situations that require and help facilitate these key attributes for competitive soccer. If emphasis is placed here during training and instruction, the players are sensitized almost inevitably to this area of character building with the appropriate guidance within the team (see chapter 1, 2, and 3). Coaches or instructors in professional soccer training should not neglect encouraging the willingness to take risks.

The following examples for practice and instruction can only become game effective when the players are willing to show a high degree of concentration and self-motivation during the training process.

The following fig. 134 shows the simulated situation of a *fake pass* from an Ajax Amsterdam player (white/blue) being confronted by the NEC Nijmegen winger (red/white) moving in and subsequently slows down his dribble, suggests a feint to the inside in the direction of the danger zone, but then makes a timed pass into the path of the trailing 10er and into the open space. This deception results in the 2-0 win against Nijmegen. This scene comes from the Dutch soccer league game from March 31, 2013, between Ajax Amsterdam and NEC Nijmegen at a 1-0 score (action sequence with times: 76:17 to 76:24 minutes of play.

Fig. 134: The fake pass in the game Ajax Amsterdam vs. NEC Nijmegen in the Dutch soccer league

EXAMPLES FOR PRACTICE AND INSTRUCTION

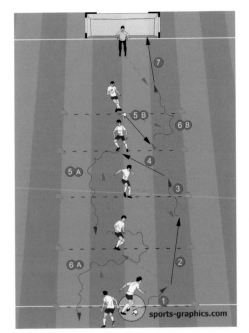

Fig. 135: Passing fakes and feints in a gird of 10—the Ajax stripes

Organization:

- Six players on a 40-x-10-m practice field.
- The practice field is divided into five equal areas and marked off with 10 cones (grid of 10). This creates a stripe pattern.
- A large goal with a goalie is positioned at a distance of approximately 16 m behind the end of the fifth stripe.
- The first and fifth players have possession. Additional balls are kept in reserve at the sides of the stripes.

Progression:

- The players are lined up behind one another.
- The third player does a pre-action to the side and gets a pass from the player at the first line (starting action by playing across the line).
- The player squares up and passes the ball to the fourth player and then chases his pass.

275

- The first and second line players simultaneously move up one line.
- The fourth player carries the ball forward (change in playing direction) and feints (including *fake pass*) and dribbles around the third, second, and first line players who have moved up.
- Meanwhile the fifth player plays a pass into the path of the third player. That player feints and dribbles around him and immediately finishes with a *one-touch shot at the large goal* with goalie with his non-dribbling foot.

Coaching:

- The third (middle) player decides to which side he will carry out the pre-action (*passing tactics*).
- Focus on playing with both feet.
- Focus on head control and keeping (*passing technique*).
- Depending on the skill level, add easements (passive, partially active) or complications (additional player moves to the outside, back, or side for 1v2) (*passing mindset*).
- Hold competitions with bonus points and ranking lists (*passing mindset*).

Variations:

- The player on the second line actively defends the pass to the third player.
- Feints with the ball with double stripe: Two adjacent stripes (18 cones, two large goals with goalies, minimum of 12 players). The two players on the first line play diagonal passes to the third line players (in each of the other stripes). They receive and carry the ball and carry out a dribble with feints (*including fake pass*) and body feints against each other. The second line players moving up generate counter-pressure at the sides, keeping heads high and doing cut-backs. After that, the progression is the same as an Ajax stripe (*passing fitness and mindset*).

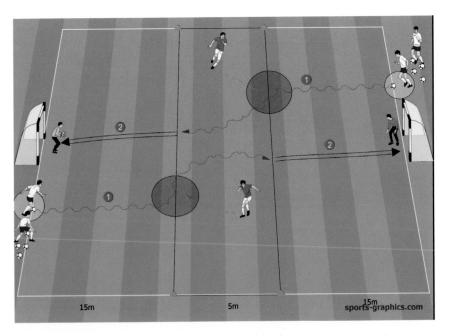

Fig. 136: Passing fakes and feints with shot at goal under spatial and counter-pressure

Organization:

- Set up two goals with goalies 35 m apart.
- Mark off a stripe or zone 5 m wide in the middle with cones. Two defenders are positioned there.
- Position additional players, depending on the desired stress level and skill level, next to the goals with one ball each.
- Keep a number of replacement balls on hand next to the goals.

Progression:

- The two players in possession signal each other, and each dribbles into the zone for the 1v1.
- The defender can only operate in the zone.
- When the attacker loses possession, he switches to the zone and defends.

Coaching:

- The defenders immediately do a fast dribble to their new starting position or pass the ball there with lots of speed and precision (changeover to offense) (*passing tactics*).

- After a turnover the attackers pursue (changeover to defense) (*passing tactics*).
- Make sure both actions start simultaneously.
- "Head up, no collisions in the zone!"
- The pace in the zone must be situational:
  1. *Fake pass* from a standing position because the space is usually very tight (see M. Götze to A. Schürrle, World Cup qualifying game on Oct. 15, 2013, Sweden vs. Germany 3-5).
  2. Fake passes at a medium pace as the most common form in 1v1 (feint and at least one alternative).
  3. Complex feinting motions at top speed are not possible. Instead suggest body feints and abrupt directional changes (goal: to overrun the opponent) (*passing intelligence and tactics*).
- "Get past the opponent and then a quick and incisive finish!" (*Passing mindset*)

Variations:

- Organize competitions:
  1. Passing fakes and feint-pro: Process with time period or number of goals to be determined.
  2. Team competitions (see 1) in which each goal scored with at least one *fake pass* in the course of the overall action up to the finish counts as triple.
  3. Biathlon-like competitions (emphasis *passing fitness*).
- Use both feet and also frequently dribble from the left (*passing technique*).
- If the goalie is able to hold on to the ball during the finish, he must throw the ball quickly and incisively into additionally mini goals. This is a way for the goalies to compete against each other (assistant or goalkeeping coach conducts this competition and together with the goalie makes the rules) (*goalie passing technique and tactics;* also see chapter 4.3.20).

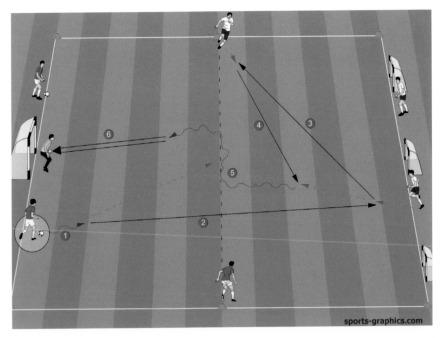

Fig. 137: Passing fakes and feints with switch passes, receiving and carrying the ball at top speed, and finishing

Organization:

- Two teams of three take turns playing 1v1 to the finish at one large goal with goalie on a playing field that is 10 x 20 m. When the defenders win the ball, a changeover game at three mini counterattacking goals ensues until a goal is scored or conceded.
- There is a minimum of seven players (including the goalie).
- Keep a number of replacement balls on hand next to the goals.

Progression:

- The player with the ball dribbles and plays a hard and incisive *flat pass* to the player opposite him. He responds with a *switch pass* to the third teammate who lets it rebound into the path of the *switch pass player*.
- He dribbles toward the goal and is pressured by the first passing player.
- In this 1v1 situation, the attacker uses *passing fakes and feints* until the finish.
- Regularly switch sides on the field.

- Attackers and defenders switch after a turnover. The *rebounders* also switch regularly.

Coaching:

- Scoring from the centerline is allowed.
- Ask for fast and incisive *flat passes* (*passing technique*).
- Receive and control the ball with a forward touch.
- Use both feet.
- Take into account the situation when choosing the pace (*passing tactics and intelligence*).

Variations:

- If the goals cause the deceptive motions and feints to not be used incisively and situationally, players can dribble *across lines* or through goals.
- Ask for *pre-actions*.
- Add a *rebounder* as
  a. an additional defender (e.g., possible double-teaming) or
  b. an additional attacker (e.g., *wall pass*, *Tiqui-Taca*, or possible *attack* in a 2v1 situation) (*passing technique and tactics*).
- Create 3v2 situations to create competitions in very tight spaces.
- 3v3 at two large goals each with goalies (*passing tactics and philosophy*).

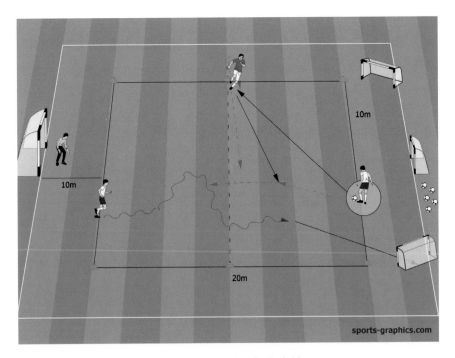

Fig. 138: Passing fakes and feints in 1v2 with three options for the finish

Organization:

- 1v2 until the finish on a 10-x-20-m playing field at one mini and two pole goals.
- The goals are set up approximately 10 m from the two head ends.
- There are at least four players (including one goalie).
- Keep a number of replacement balls handy next to the goals.

Progression:

- The player with the ball plays *a wall pass* with the outer teammate and directs the rebounded ball with a *one-touch pass* out of the *post-action* to the player opposite him.
- He receives and controls the pass while moving and dribbles toward the goal.
- The dribbling player and the *wall pass players* are pressured from the front and the side.
- In this 1v2 situation the attacker uses *passing fakes and feints* until the finish.
- After a turnover the goal scorer of the superior number team switches with

the attacker. The *rebounder's* and *wall pass-player's* positions are also switched regularly.

- When the two defenders gain possession, changeover play at a large goal with goalie ensues until a goal is scored or conceded.

Coaching:

- Goals can be scored from the head ends.
- Ask for quick and incisive *flat passes* (*passing technique*).
- Receive and carry the ball with a forward touch.
- Pay attention to the situation when choosing the pace (*passing tactics and intelligence*).
- "Both opponents are too slow in position: Quickly run past them or overrun them! Don't get outmaneuvered!" (*Passing tactics*)
- "Both opposing players are positioned too far apart: Use *passing fakes and feints* and through the gap, keep up the pace, and finish!" (*Passing tactics*)
- "Physical play!" (*Passing fitness*)

Variations:

- If the goals cause the deceptive motions and feints to not be used incisively and situationally, players can dribble *across lines* or through *through-goals*
- Easements for the single player:
  a. Outnumbered player can take the shot at goal from the centerline.
  b. Position passers between the goals and the head end (*rebounders*).
- Ask for pre-actions.
- Play with both feet.
- Start competitions: Pass-faker of the day (with prizes or rewards).

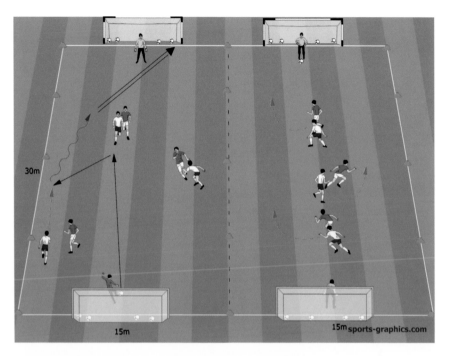

Fig. 139: Passing fakes and feints for 3v3 plus goalie—It's all about the axial positions!

Organization:

- Four teams play 3v3 plus goalies at two large goals on adjacent fields that are 30 x 15 m.
- Keep lots of replacement balls handy next to the goals.

Progression:

- Players on the right field initially position in a triple axis with central defender, midfielder, and forward. From these positions, the goalie initiates the following action (see left playing field). The team in possession initiates mirror-inverted fanning out.
- Players on the left field are holding their lines, are already fanning out, and are preparing for a pass from the goalie (offering support and getting open). The goalie typically chooses the *long pass* (a) to the forward. He lets the ball *rebound* to the right to the central defender after a previous *fake pass* to the left. This player receives the pass at a high rate of speed and tries to affect a prompt finish.

Coaching:

- Depending on axis position, position and ability of the opponent, positions and ability of teammates (including goalie): sole inside turn, sole outside turn, standing, carrying the ball to the side or back at a diagonal, *rebounding, fake passes, penetrating.*

- The goalies must execute additional game openers: (b) Pass to the midfielder (second axis); (c) pass to the central defender.

Variations:

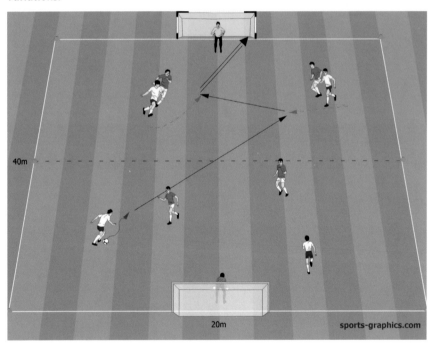

Fig. 140: Passing fakes and feints for 4v4 plus goalie—staggered depth and width

Organization:

- Two pairs of players plus a goalie in each zone (40 x 20 m total) at two large goals.

Progression:

- 2v2 against 2v2 until the finish.

Coaching:

- Attackers are staggered in depth and width (e.g., *Deep-lying* forward ties up defender on the outside, looks for cooperation from his partner and after the pass lets the ball *rebound* to the second forward playing with the third man, who finishes). Alternatives: Fake pass, sole outside turn in playing direction and 1v1.

Fig. 141: Passing fakes and feints for 5v5 plus goalies—triple axis with 9er and two wingers

Organization:

- 5v5 plus goalies at two large goals on one half of a field.

Progression:

- 5v5 until the finish.

Coaching:

- Take up positions: Triple axis with central defender (4er), midfielder (6er), and forward (9er), plus 2 wingers (7er and 11er); getting open (here deep-lying on the right 7er, coordinate 6er halfway on the right, and the 9er with *running feint*).
- "Don't start in the same spaces!"

4.3.20 GOALIE PASSING SPECIAL WITH GOALKEEPER TRAINER MARCO KNOOP (RB LEIPZIG)

"School was out at 3:40 pm, and at 4:15 I had to be on the field ready to play. Back then all I did was play soccer. We had ten, twelve practices during the week and a game on the weekend. That was my life and I loved being on the field. That hasn't changed one bit."

(International goalie, Bayern Munich goalie and Goalkeeper of the Year Manuel Neuer, April 7, 2014, in *kicker*, pg. 11)

Marco Knoop has been goalkeeper trainer of the U23-U16 at RB Leipzig (see photo) since July 2013.

He is a DFB-A licensee and a certified sport scientist. He served as coach at the DFB base camp Bochum from 2004-2006 and goalkeeper trainer for the VfL Bochum 1848 youth division from 2006-2013.

In addition to his extensive practical experience in competitive soccer's goalkeeper training, Marco Knoop also possesses enormous knowledge in the area of elite sports training and kinematics and has been published on the goalkeeping as well as given lectures at BDFL and DFB conferences.

4.3.20.1 FACTS ABOUT MODERN GOALKEEPING

This chapter focuses on the goalkeeper position as an active component at the game's opening and continued play from Marco Knoop's point of view. The standard situation of a penalty kick from the goalie's perspective does not relate to the topics chosen by us. We, therefore, refer the interested reader to the appropriate sources (Kibele 2013, pg. 46-54; Neumaier/te Poel and Standtke 1987, pg. 23-32). The classification of modern goalkeeping is based above all else on the findings of current sport science research that objectively shows that the position-specific requirement profile for the training of today's goalkeepers has fundamentally changed[15].

The language in this chapter has also been consciously chosen to incorporate some goalkeeping-specific vocabulary into text and images. This is intended to add greater authenticity for the practical and theoretical use with *goalkeeper passing*.

In the unabridged German version of this book, Marco Knoop introduces modern goalkeeping drills starting with the U15 performance range. These drills should be viewed as creative food for thought for coaches and instructors for diverse and effective goalkeeper training on the field.

That the goalkeeper has a special function in a game is probably beyond dispute. He is a special type of player who is not only dressed differently and gets to hold the ball with his hands, but he also raises the tempers of spectators much more intensely and longer with just a single error. On the other hand, a successful action is viewed as rather normal. In this respect, goalkeeper training that focuses on further development in the sense of the overall concept of this book (see chapter 4.3) should include the areas of *mindset* and *personality*.

---

15   To the interested reader we additionally recommend the current published works of David Thiel (goalkeeper with Bayer 04 Leverkusen) (2012, pg. 7-19), DFB sports coach Jörg Daniel on set pieces (2013, pg. 34-41), Marten Arts of the Netherlands (2013, pg. 32-37), Thomas Schlieck (formerly with Arminia Bielefeld and FC Schalke 04, presently with RB Leipzig) (in Hyballa and te Poel, 2013, pg. 132-139), and the DVD standard works by DFB goalkeeper trainer of the national team, Andreas Köpke (Goalkeeping School with Andreas Köpke, part 1, and Professional Goalkeeping, part 2 with Andreas Köpke)

> *"A goalie is 75% of the game. Except if he is a bad goalie. Then it is 100%."*
>
> (Gene Ubriaco quoted by Jochen Reimer in The Red Bulletin magazine, September, 2013 issue).

The quality of the defense's final man can have a critical impact on the outcome of the game. The goalie's basic defensive actions, such as saving or deflecting flat balls into the corner of the goal or in 1v1 situations, require a specialist. The extent of the goalie's soccer abilities, skills, techniques, and tactics is becoming increasingly important and sometimes makes the difference between a mediocre and an excellent keeper, particularly in today's competitive soccer.

In the recent past, several scientific studies on the goalkeeper's playing requirements have been published. While the results are not entirely surprising to a soccer expert, they do put the ratio of defensive to offensive actions of today's goalies up for discussion (see Ferrauti, Pischetsrieder, Knoop and Streibig 2009). At the 2008 Men's European Championships, 20 top international goalkeepers demonstrated the following goalkeeping behavior.

Tab. 1: Number (absolute and percent) of defensive and offensive actions of selected top goalkeepers at the 2008 Men's European Championships (emphasis on probability of safe arrival during the goalkeepers' offensive actions)

Average number of goalies' defensive actions:	approx. 15-20
Average number of offensive actions:	approx. 25-35
Probability of safe arrival of offensive actions (in %):	
Passes, long and high:	30%
Passes, short and flat:	98%
Goal kicks/free kicks, long and high:	31%
Goal kicks/free kicks, short and flat:	97%
Punts hand, long and high:	24%
Throw-out/*roll-out*, short and long:	100%

During a game the goalie, using the example of analyses from the 2008 Men's European Championships (see tab. 1), is confronted more often with offensive than defensive actions overall.

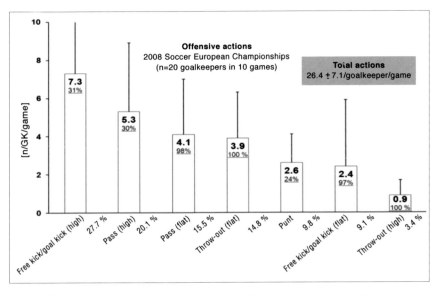

Fig. 142: Offensive actions with goalkeeper passes at the 2008 Men's European Championships (see Ferrauti, Pischetsrieder, Knoop and Streibig)

Three principles for opening and continuing the game can be taken from these descriptive analyses under the premise of continued possession and given to the coach or instructor to bring to training:

1. HAND BEFORE FOOT	2. SHORT BEFORE LONG
3. FLAT BEFORE HIGH	

Additional studies by Thaler and Krebs (2009, pg. 20-29) on the 2007/2008 season (229 goalkeeping analyses of 51 goalies from 1st and 2nd Division Bundesliga) and the 2008 Men's European Championships (62 games) provide similar results. They even make a case for replacing the present term *goalkeeper* with *goalplayer* in the future. As can be seen in the following information, this new positional designation, also known in soccer under the motto "the goalie as Libero," requires more differentiated analysis and subsequent mediation.

The study by Thaler and Krebs (2009) divides goalkeeper behavior into four main actions and stresses the three principles of modern soccer mentioned previously:

Tab. 2: The four main actions of a goalkeeper (as per Thaler and Krebs 2009)

Defensive actions (hand and foot) strictly to prevent a goal:	9%
Playing actions (hand and foot) in and outside of the box:	39%
Goal kicks/free kicks:	31%
Continuing the game after receiving the ball:	21%

The study by Rechner and Memmert (pg. 32) published in 2010 expands on these findings as it includes and analyzes players from the English Premiere League and the Spanish Primera Division from 2008 and 2009. The study provides the following results.

Tab. 3: Percentages of defensive and offensive goalkeeper actions during the evaluated games (as per Rechner and Memmert 2010)

Goal defense (shots, headers, 1v1)	approx. 15%
Space defense (crosses/any kind of ball into the box and floaters)	approx. 10%
Foot play/opening the game (throw outs, punts, goal kicks, back pass processing, and clearings)	approx. 75%

In recent years, when tracking the empirical findings regarding the goalkeeper's modified requirements profile in today's professional soccer, priorities and variances with respect to method content within modern and sustainable goalkeeper training (and thus the daily training processes) must change (see chapter 4.5). While the authors classify all of the actions of modern goalkeeping as such, with the exception of deflecting balls with hands, arms, and trunk, *goalkeeper passing* plays a central role in everyday goalkeeper training.

"Whenever the Bayern or German national team is on the ball Manuel Neuer also plays. He is good at initiating plays, quickly initiates counterattacks, and he is far outside the goal when there is a high line in front of him. Over the years Manuel has learned to recognize when the situation is right for him to come out of the goal. He senses: Where must I stand? When can I come out? When can I come way out? Of course he has made mistakes in the course of his career, but this style of playing is important. In today's soccer goalkeepers who can take on the part of Libero are in demand. Manuel is always ready for a pass, which gives his team an advantage in the back. He thereby meets the requirements for a modern goalkeeper perfectly because the goalkeeper game has changed."

(Joachim Löw, German national team coach, March 10, 2014, in kicker, pg. 6)

These necessary changes in the training of soccer goalkeepers also result in a change in the goalie's position within the team (*passing philosophy*, see chapter 4.1). What does that really mean? If, for instance, a coach asks his team to play *short passes* (see chapter 4.3.6) to accomplish a high possession rate, a goalkeeper, after having received the *back pass*, usually has multiple short- and medium-distance passing options because of the active demands of his teammates. He must adapt to and get involved in these situations.

But if a coach brings a (*playing*) *philosophy* to the club that focuses on winning the *first or even second ball* to surprise the disorganized opponent moving forward, the goalie would be required to play a large number of incisive and long *goalkeeper passes*. Training the passing game therefore closely correlates with the (*playing*) *philosophy* of the coach or instructor and the team.

Today's modern goalkeeper training is responsible for training goalkeepers in such a way that they can appropriately participate in defensive and offensive team play.

Here, too, it becomes clear that isolated and largely technique-oriented goalkeeping training is no longer enough for becoming an elementary part of the team with its key performance factors, requirements, and playing philosophies (see chapters 1 and 3).

Digression: As we have already determined, continued possession by the own team after the game opener or continued play usually depends on the three principles: Hand before foot, short before long, flat before high. Using the example of the German national team goalie Manuel Neuer's throw-out behavior we want to explain why this technique can be of such great importance and plays such a critical role for the team and the implementation of the playing philosophy in the goalkeeper Passing Puzzle. When he quickly switched to offensive action after intercepting a cross, his incisive long throw-outs—in some cases more than 65 yards—allowed him to speed up the entire team's game by an extreme amount and thereby put pressure (physical and mental) on the opposing team. Passing the ball by hand can therefore be considered an actual pass because these passes (rolling, hurling, punting) send the same message to the teammates as passes with the foot: "I want to play with you! Here is a quality ball; do something with it!" Moreover the pass by hand can be done much more accurately than by foot, and the ball can't be stolen as long as the goalie holds it in his hands. So the execution can take place without time pressure, which clearly increases the success rate.

In view of that fact, during the selection of drills, training exercises were chosen that include continuation of play with a pass by hand.

4.3.20.2 KEY POINTS ABOUT GOALKEEPER PASSING

The forms of training conceived by Marco Knoop primarily focus on *short passes* and passes bridging *medium distances* within the goalie-specific passing game (referred to as *goalkeeper passing*). To make the quality of the goalie-specific passing game as effective as possible through training, we will at this point present a condensed version of some goalie-specific elements for *coaching* and *methods* during training units with goalkeepers (see tab. 4). Further methodological suggestions can be found in chapter 4.5.

Tab. 4: Goalkeeper coaching: Keywords and codes in modern goalkeeper training

Use as few touches as possible, but as many as are necessary to keep up the pace.
Actively ask for the ball, signal availability to receive the ball (verbal: "Play!" and "Open hand, where?")
Create a comfortable distance to the opponent by offsetting width and depth.
Use precision and dosed hardness to create a time cushion for the open man to process the pass.
First touch should be in playing direction so that the second touch can be well prepared and no emergency solution (clearance) is required.
Avoid the ball coming to a dead stop.
Play simple passes (angle less than 90 degrees to the passer and receiver).
Form triangles to avoid passing across the supporting leg (loss of speed due to spin).
Thoughtless low-quality passes create pressure for the receiver (e.g., A clumsy pass to the central defender). Remember: His problem will become your problem when the central defender panics and plays an uncontrolled return pass.
Avoid balls with topspin as they are difficult to process because they are rough.
Balls to the central defender should always be played to the man and ideally to the strong foot with instruction ("Cut!" or "Rebound!").
Play balls to the 6er only when he is unchallenged, and then flat to the foot and with instruction.
Balls to the wingback or the wide central defender should be played to the offensive foot (foot in playing direction) and offer support if he does not cut outside.
Immediately after winning the ball or before a return pass scan the field for options. First look goes deep, second one wide, third one short, and fourth strike if necessary (*safety first principle*).
Be respectful in your actions (don't humiliate the opponent and don't play for time).

Do not cross that fine line from courage to rashness by overinterpreting the active mindset. After all you wear the "1" and not the "10." Preventing goals is the top priority.

The coach can train and modify the following drills by using certain pressure regulators with varying degrees of difficulty. This can also shift the presented training priority. The following pressure factors can be useful in practical goalkeeper training.

PRESSURE OF TIME

Practical example: Counting down. When does the action have to be finished?

PRESSURE OF PRECISION

Practical example: Choose relatively small target goals or set them up far apart.

SITUATIONAL PRESSURE

Practical example: Use provocation rules or sanctions and bonuses.

PRESSURE OF COMPLEXITY

Practical examples: Create information overload through multitasking.

PRESSURE OF STRESS

Practical examples: Due to prior physical or mental fatigue.

The professional application of the depicted pressure regulators is based on the Neumaier model (1999). It is referred to as the Coordination Requirements Regulator Model and will not be elaborated on here (see Neumaier and Bush).

4.4 THE HYBALLA/TE POEL PASSING PHILOSOPHY

"Of course we would make fewer mistakes if we had the ball less often. If we didn't want to play, but rather just knock the ball forward. But I don't like that kind of coincidental soccer."

(Bert van Marwijk, former head coach Hamburger SV and national team coach of the vice world champions the Netherlands, quoted in the *Frankfurter Allgemeine Zeitung*, Nov. 11, 2013)

The coach's point of view:

"It is absolutely necessary to find a clear-cut course and to make it perfectly understood. Every player on the squad needs to understand the coach's philosophy. This requires definite agreements. And the coach must play by these rules and enforce their adherence. Otherwise he will have a problem."

(Jos Luhukay, head coach Hertha BSC, quoted in *kicker*, Sept. 9, 2013)

The player's point of view:

"Most important is that the team has the right spirit. That everyone is willing to go the extra mile for the other, defensively and offensively. When the mind and the spirit and the passion are in it, that's half the battle. The rest, the tactical, that just fine-tunes everything and brings it closer to perfection."

(Thomas Müller, player on the German national team and FC Bayern Munich, from an interview with Christian Kamp in the *Frankfurter Allgemeine Zeitung*, Oct. 10, 2014, pg. 24)

But what does a *passing and playing philosophy* actually look like, and how can it be communicated to the players? To answer this question, we use the *Hyballa/te Poel* (*passing*) *philosophy* for a professional team as an example (also see chapter 4.1).

1. Attack is the ticket with a narrow 1-4-3-3! Passing is the first choice because the ball is faster than a dribbling player, and we have lots of triangles. Please note: Before you get the ball you should already have a plan what to do with it! Avoid square passes. (*Passing line*)

2. Pressing begins in the front. The forward signals for the pressing to start: "We want to regain possession right away to continue to execute 1!" Therefore, win the ball with "airbag" safety and then charge forward.

3. Opening the game, building up, and finishing: Tempo with the own attack. No time-consuming cross-field play without gaining space, but rather putting pressure on the opponent early with dribbling and long passes: passing relays and constant position changes can wear the opponent down physically and mentally. Lightning fast changes in speed and direction give the attackers direct scoring opportunities. Central defenders should force the opposing forward out of their space with targeted dribbling. Whoever dribbles or has to dribble because he doesn't see another option creates open space for his teammates that can be passed into. The wingbacks should therefore not *swing out* to the sidelines because that only leaves them options along the line. If they move farther in, they are able to operate inside, forward, and outside. The pass to the center usually reaches the 6er in a *half-open* position or with his back to the opposing goal. He, too, must immediately attack, and if necessary *open up* into playing direction. The 10 position plays a very important role here (e.g., in the previously mentioned 1-4-3-3 with point in back). This player either dribbles toward the goal or tries to play through one of the three forwards. The forwards also look for the short way to the goal with a 1v1. The option of a wing attack always remains open. Crosses are mostly played flat because flat balls are easier to process than waist-high or high balls.

4. Position training: Specify the grammar—in other words, dribbling, passing, *opening up, starting*, and getting open for the attacking game. Positional discipline with tactical problems for defensive play.

"Of course each position comes with a strategic task. Tactics are most important in the area of defense because all parts must work together, and we have to be able to rely on each other. The system has to function. Offensive play can be a little loser. Here it is more about creativity, the element of surprise, the unexpected. A rigid system would be a hindrance here."

(Thomas Müller, player on the German national team and FC Bayern Munich, from an interview with Christian Kamp in the Frankfurter Allgemeine Zeitung, Oct. 10, 2013, pg. 24.)

5. Set priorities within a form of play and coach situationally. Example:

   Safe buildup:

   - Central defender dribbles into the next zone or *flat passes* to 6/8.
   - Skip the next zone with a pass (*pass into space*); no return passes into the respective back zone.
   - Determine the number of mandatory stations per zone (holding on to the ball).
   - *Shot at goal* for the finish from a specific zone (short pass or *skip over*).
   - team competitions: Team A against Team B with different guidelines for the buildup.

6. The current game analyses play a large part in determining training content.

7. Use forms of play to enter into training. Offer interesting and motivational training, particularly in youth training.

Hyballa giving instructions to the U-19 Leverkusen team

4.5 THE METHODOLOGY KEY: HOW TO TRAIN THE PASSING PUZZLE IQ®

"Sometimes I can't believe that there are people who really believe that muscles work on their own."

(Hans-Dieter Hermann, staff sports psychologist for the German national soccer team, in Memmert, Strauss & Theweleit 2013, pg. 27)

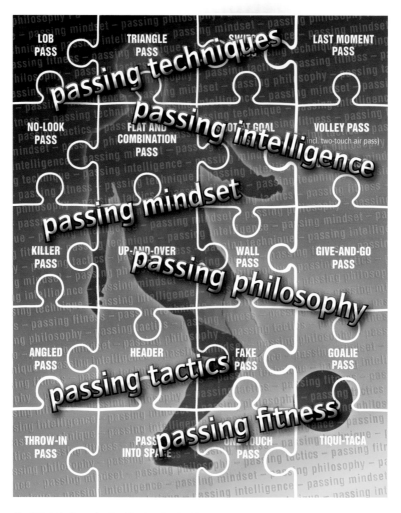

Fig. 143: Hyballa and te Poel Passing Puzzle IQ®

When combining the individual puzzles from chapters 4.3.1 to 4.3.20 and underpinning them with those performance-determining factors in soccer that we consider essential (see chapter 4.1), the question from the coach and instructor as well as the players immediately arises: How do I put these important contents into practice during training and instruction?

Entire libraries and digital compendiums are filled with answers to the question: How do I impart and train my most important content with my players? The assumption that trainability in today's soccer of technique optimization (for modern passing game training) is possible between the ages of 10 and 59 and the learning rate is steady is an empirically-backed finding (see Wollny 2002).

The *golden age of learning* in youth training does not exist because training playing techniques extends to the entire playing career (see Roth 2005b, pg. 339).

The target level for systematic technique training in soccer looks as follows (see Roth 2005b, pg. 336-337):

1. The phase of learning something new with attentive scrutiny.
2. The phase of overlearning with increasing scrutiny.
3. The phase of automation of individual technical sections accompanied by attention to technical optimization.
4. The phase of stabilization and variability in the execution of techniques with focus on solving open problems with the goal of gaining skills by result.

The method of levels in systematic technical training is based on the classification into four target areas (Roth 2005b, pg. 338-339):

1. The phase of using simplification strategies (e.g., rhythm and orientation aids, practicing in slow motion, minimal exertion)
2. A short phase of repeating techniques.
3. The phase of adding additional strategic challenges (see Szymanski 1997), with

the goal of speeding up the automation processes by diverting attention (with additional strategic tasks).

4. The phase of changing the basic patterns by directing freed up attention (e.g., with variable practice and random tasks and always combined with methods of technical stabilization).

When looking at the goals and methods that allow the *Hyballa & te Poel Passing Puzzle IQ®* training content to efficiently take effect over time (and divided into the learning phases of a consortium) in the sense of allowing learning to efficiently take effect, many open questions emerge:

- With respect to **technique training** (keyword *passing technique*), these ranges between the poles problem-oriented learning and theme-centered interaction involve considerations from research on general and differential motor function (keywords playing and practicing), and system-theoretical and action-oriented argumentation (see Roth 2005b). A current study on training science by Voigt/ Hohmann and Singh (2013, pg. 4-15) on subjective training theories regarding the competitive sports training process in game sports confirms the theory that more research is required in which methods should primarily be used during levels of technical training. In view of the fact that most coaches and instructors in game sports focus primarily on the sport's basic technical elements in, for instance, youth sports, this represents on the one hand a central challenge and responsibility to all parties concerned (see Voigt/Hohmann and Singh 2013, pg.7). "Thus the long-term technical training strategy ranges between a permanent area of conflict between the demand for perspectival, versatile training and developmental training design, and on the other hand the timely creation of a highly developed ability to compete based on specific motor programs" (see Voigt/Hohmann and Singh 2013, pg.7). Furthermore recent technical innovations are becoming more popular with professional clubs, youth soccer centers, and camps. Two examples of this are the Footbonaut (training center for technical training at BV Borussia Dortmund 09) and Quick Feet (individual passing and receiving training system designed by inventor and FA coach Chris McGinn). However neither system has received a sport-scientific evaluation at this time.

> *"Correcting mistakes is the most important technological and learning method overall. It appears to be the only method for progress in biological evolution. The terms method, trial and error are justified, but in doing so one underestimates the importance of a wrong conclusion or mistake – of the flawed attempt [...] All of life is solving problems."*
>
> (Popper 1995, pg. 256-257)

- There is still much research needed in the area of **tactical skills** training (keyword passing tactics) with respect to the efficiency of training methods for performance (see Roth 2005c), and the inconsistent points of view among game sports coaches on combining game-situational training of individual players—keyword individualization (example 2013 BDFL [Association of German Soccer Instructors] conference)—with a team's collective tactical style of play (see Voigt/Hohmann & Singh 2013, pg. 13).

- In the area of **game sports conveyance** there is the question of the optimal relationship between implicit and explicit appropriation processes, which also applies to the ambiguous statements regarding the frequently applied policies "playing and practicing" and "playing before practicing" (see Roth 2005a):

> *"There is a lack of entities for the continued development of players. We still talk about training teams. But training must include practice, not just application."*
>
> (Marcus Sorg, coach U19 German national team, at the introduction of the UEFA Youth League in the *Frankfurter Allgemeine Zeitung*, Sept. 17, 2013, pg. 29)

- However in practical training and instruction *technique training* cannot be planned and executed without assessing the correlation between **fitness training and technique training** (keyword *passing fitness*). This also applies to the level of individual strain in collective soccer training and instruction. Temporal coordination of the development of individual form presents a prospect for continuing research in the future. There are still many open questions in this area.

- **Complex training**, a magic word for every modern type of training and instruction? The *complex training* approach links coordinative, technical, tactical, and mental factors (keyword *passing intelligence*). It is very competition-like, is geared toward improving performance factors in game-like contexts, is intended to effect temporization, and increases motivation (see Memmert 2005, pg. 360). To what extent mental and physical strain during actual competitions can be replicated in competition-oriented training is still unclear and debated.

- Is the **accent method** provided by the block-by-block training of performance factors an effective means for learning-based (vs. intentional) training processes (see Frey & Hildenbrandt 1995, pg. 110)?

- When adding the **coaching** factor (see Seeger 2008; Bechthold 2014, pg. 22-26; Merz & Thiel 2014, pg. 39-45) whose goal it is to "achieve the highest-possible degree of competition and action readiness via optimal focus and motivation during competitive play" (Seeger 2008, pg. 9)? We have come full circle back to chapters 2,3, and 4:

> *For the chosen topics we provide a somewhat simplistic link between the passing mindset and the target areas communication and interaction ("Learning to understand each other!"), action, motivation, self-confidence, attitude, and the players' emotional state as key aspects within a pass[16]. Self-efficacy and collective action are not mutually exclusive.*

Since many coaches and instructors consider the importance of disciplined play, stress stability, and the necessity of one or possible multiple leaders in U17 to U21 teams to be crucial to successful competitive play, coaching with unimpeded communication plays a central role (see Voigt/Hohmann & Singh 20113, pg. 13; Bechthold & Otto

---

16 At this point in the learning process some special consideration must be given to the standards and parts of the goalkeeper's game because their effectiveness is primarily subject to the development of stable motor problem-solving methods or variable coping patterns for closed and slightly open tasks (see chapter 4.3.20).

2014, pg. 22-27). How can this be implemented in the field? Next to motivational measures during practice and games such as praise, incentive, encouragement, volition training, and stamina, that are often forgotten in professional soccer, the following two examples from our own training and competition practice can help positional groups orient themselves appropriately on the field using previously agreed upon fixed code words:

*1. Example for **situational coaching** among players:*

- "No opponent at the back? Open up!"
- "Opponent at the back? One-touch pass!"
- "Behind the opponent? Pre-action: Get out of the cover shadow!"
- "Pass into space? Post-action: Go with the ball!"
- "Tight space, opponent presses? Tiqui-Taca, give-and-go passes and rebounds, or triangle passes!"
- "Get out of a tight space? Deep and wide switch passes!"

The previously mentioned agreements are implemented vocally, through gestures, eye contact, body language, and behavioral responses, and their appropriateness must be pondered continuously.

*2. Example for helping each other during practice and competition by **determining specific codes.***

CODES FOR FIELD PLAYERS:

"Open!" or *"Time!"* (You are able to dribble, shoot, or pass without interference from the opponent!)

"Man!" (Watch out, the opponent is already close to you!)

"Coming!" (Watch out, opponent is approaching!)

"Run!" or *"Pressure!"* (Go to the ball, I've got your back!)

"Pass forward!" or *"Through!"* (Play a long ball!)

"Open up!" (Quickly turn in playing direction!)

"Chip!" (Play a short but well-directed fly ball with spin)!

"Dribble!" (Dribble when you can't pass or shoot!)

"Fire!" (Pick up the pace!)

"Tiqui-Taca!" (Hold on to the ball, slow it down!)

"Bounce! and Turn!" (Play the ball right back to me, turn quickly, and get open!)

"Move up!" (Quickly close up to the front line!)

"Switch!" (Swiftly play the ball to other side of the field by switching sides!)

"Let it go!" (You can let the ball go past your supporting leg, no opponent near you!)

"Close the middle!" (Players on the off-ball side must move toward the center!)

"Help!" (Offer support so the player in possession can pass easily!)

CODE WORDS FOR GOALKEEPERS:

"Leo!" (Shout from the goalie when he feels his players need to let the ball go.)

"Here!" (Shout from the goalie when the ball must be played back because he is not coming out of the goal.)

"Go to!" (Shout from the goalie when he does not come out of the goal with a high ball but rather wants the players to engage in an air duel; possibly combined with a name.)

■ A detailed description of the **passing philosophy** was already provided in chapter 4.4 via the "own plan." Before it is implemented in the field with the aid of team psychological methods and techniques for practical use (see Baumann 2008), this plan should be introduced to the team, the support staff, the BOD/supervisory committee, established fan groups, the press, and the sponsors. If the plan and its objectives are understood and even accepted it clearly adds to its improved functional cohesion, contentment, and social cohesion (Baumann 2008, pg. 62). Because with the implementation of the present *Hyballa/te Poel Passing Puzzle IQ®* all participants also or particularly want diversion and to experience something special, without having to abandon the tried and true. But that requires mutual trust and multiple heads.

Success cannot be planned, but performance can with a coach or instructor and one's own environment!

Because of limited publication a more detailed description of the team psychological rules and techniques for effective implementation of the passing philosophy cannot be included here.

In our attempt to structure and systemize, the *beginner training* will be excluded from our modern passing game and will be presented elsewhere from the point of view of a school that teaches ball games. This also applies to the areas of *mental coaching*, *leadership styles*, and the substantial debate started by the German Dr. Phil. (kinesiology) W.I. Schöllhorn on the customary system of principles in training and the presentation of an alternative approach that includes standards from science theory (see Schöllborn, Beckmann and Michelbrink 2013, pg. 5-10).

The notion that particularly technical and tactical content should be combined in the learning process in game sports and combat sports (see Szymanski 1997; Roth 2005a, b, and c; Wormuth 2011 and 2013) is currently beyond dispute in game sport research and top-level soccer. On the other hand, based

on findings from the psychology of action and teaching psychology Wahl (2012, pg. 55) points out that learning through playing "[...] should be supplemented by selectively interspersed phases of explicit learning" so the learners are able to "organize" their actions.

This does not only help to better read a game but also to anticipate externally and internally, to make better decisions under time pressure, and to monitor the execution of movements more consciously. The former DFB head instructor Erich Rutemöller already transferred this approach to fitness training in soccer in 2010 (pg. 40), and the coaching instructor and athletic director of the DFB youth program Jörg Daniel currently continues this approach via basic games for learning techniques that preserve complexity and motivation, but also facilitate the grinding in of the movements.

His valuation parameters for the selection and use of basic forms of play using the example of a training unit in the sequence of warm up, main part (basic forms of play alternating with drills or short forms) and closing (4v4 tournament or final game) are

- proven suitability for practical use and
- fun (Rutemöller, pg. 52-53).

But the established deficiencies in research and the associated open questions regarding the overall effectiveness of many methodical suggestions on the topic will not prevent the authors from giving a nuanced presentation of *methods and rules of teaching training* for the *modern passing game* and to categorize according to their priorities and their affinity for the training and teaching goal: *motor, cognitive, and mixed (linked)*. They refer to the individual puzzle pieces and their correlation with the selected performance factors *technique, tactics (including passing intelligence), and fitness (stamina)*.

Unsorted and fragmented descriptions of *teaching methods and rules* along with bibliographical references for continuing self-guided studies (see tab. 5) can be found in the following chart.

Using the same metaphor as in chapters 2, 3, and 4, coaches and instructors should critically contemplate this framework with respect to the specific requirements of their team or group, correlate it with the *coaching elements* and the *variations* in chapters 4.3.1-4.2.20, and create customized learning processes based on their own experiences.

> *"Roughly 55% of all goals are not random. Thus the greater part of a team's fortune still rests in its own feet."*
> (Memmert, Strauss & Theweleit 2013, pg. 97)

Bayern Munich coach Pep Guardiola (right) during training with his player Bastian Schweinsteiger

Tab. 5: Teaching methods and rules for training the modern passing game

For the motor component:	For the cognitive component:	Mixed forms (including the fitness and video feedback components):
Repetition method	Methods for the use of supplementary methods (e.g., to control movement perception and to convey technomotor correlations; choosing the push pass technique for incisive *short passes*).	Presenting multiple challenges in the area of player's abilities (cognitive, coordinative, and fitness-related) (see Weineck, Memmert & Uhing 2012).
Method for the variation of practice conditions (e.g., number of players, size of playing field, materials, environmental factors, time limits, touch limit, rules) including contrasting tasks (e.g., constantly changing distances to the goal).	Methods for the use of internal feedback (e.g., via kinesthetic tasks) and repetition and verbal agreements (group and team tactics).	Training based on typical game conditions.
Examining the new and the proven.	Use of compelling learning aids (e.g., decreasing the size of the playing field, panels, and using modern audio visual materials).	Training under competition-like conditions and more difficult variations of competition-like conditions (e.g., under physical stress, see Oliver 1996).
Reducing feedback frequency (see Wulf and Prinz 2001).	Use of *small-sided games* (basic games) (e.g., 4v4 at mini goals or in the soccer stadium with arranged situations) (see Wein 2004; Memmert 2012b).	Tournaments, internal championships, rankings, awards, prizes, and various forms of appreciation.
Alternating skills..	Basic games with inferior and superior numbers (see Memmert 2006).	Provocation rules—goal advantage, special zones, special players with positional tasks, multiple points, limits (e.g., team touches), handicaps, no coaching, player coaching.

Confronting professional goals and skills.	Provocation rules and tournaments, habituation methods (familiarization): Entering into situations that have been frightening with the goal of understanding the underlying mechanisms (e.g., 89th minute of playing time with a 0-1 score: Deciding between a risky *killer pass* or a *combination pass* that will delay a decision). Using positive emotions to convey, or rather produce, a feeling that the type of pass a player just successfully completed is important to the present aspirations: highest quality passes. Training volition—following through with decision (shifting play) and action (*switch pass*). Goal: Confident action by building necessary neural networks in the brain.	Use of indoor tournaments with specific focus areas (e.g., futsal tournaments) and variation on *passing techniques* and implementation requirements.
Maximal variations of goals, execution speeds, and techniques (see Schöllhorn et al. 2006; Hegen and Schöllhorn 2012a and b).	Recognizing and correcting erroneous decisions with the aid of video analysis: Situational changing of chosen techniques.	Players participate in planning training content and locations as well as playing locations and modes (e.g., beach soccer, lawn soccer, street soccer)
Teamwork with the technical coach using a block system (see Hordijk 2012).	Developing thoughtful application to optimize technical precision using video analyses and conversations about technique and tactics and the tactics-oriented video confrontation method for the areas of playing discipline and stability.	Video feedback with the aid of different technologies (see Novoisky et al. 2012; Lames 2012).

---

17 *Bei Anteilnahme positiver Emotionen übermitteln Botenstoffe Informationen zwischen den Neuronen, die so näher zusammen rücken, sodass Impulse leichter übertragen werden können und den Prozess der Erweiterung neuronaler Strukturen begünstigen (vgl. u.a. G. Roth 2009).*

Planning the season with thematic blocks (see Hehl 2014).	Team play training: • Training for the development of alternative solutions: counterfactual thinking. • Team debriefing. • Video self-confrontation. • Video self-confrontation in individual situations • Gaining different points of view (see Hänsel and Baumgärtner 2014).	Game-appropriate coaching—maturity, emotional control, positive thinking, addressing the individual, adequate pressure, form of address, conversation at the sideline, agreeing on codes, coaching during practice (e.g., freeze-frame and practical demonstration), and using half-times for targeted feedback (see Bechthold and Otto 2014, pg. 26-27; Linz 2006).

Basic games are particularly valuable for promoting creativity in soccer (see fig. 144 and center column), especially in youth soccer. The cognitive and sport scientist Dr. D. Memmert (2012b, pg. 28) talks about the five Ds of promoting creativity and suggests the following content and methodical approach.

One-dimension games:

Basis modular games can teach individual basic techniques from many game sports via numerous similar recurring situational constellations.

Diversification:

Using different motor skills in basis modular games can help to form original variations to solutions.

Deliberate coaching:

No instructions should be used in the basis modular games that diminish the attention and focus of the participants.

Deliberate play:

Acting without directions in the basis modular games can result in trying out different kinds of solutions.

Deliberate motivation:

Hope-based instructions that generate more unusual solutions should be used in the basis modular games.

Fig. 144: The five Ds for promoting creativity in game sports

The key to a modern passing game fits into the lock and can be used any time in many different ways. It is intended to help a player and all others involved to sort and to optimize different thoughts and approaches to end up with an improved scope of experience. This takes extensive and intensive work overall (game!) as well as the details, much time, patience, persistence, and understanding for the different behaviors of people in the process, conceptual work, and lots of faith from everyone in its success. And finally, a word of wisdom from the previously mentioned Heidelberg game sports scientist:

"Anyone who has to run 100 m should consider 90 m to be halfway!"

(Roth 2005b, pg. 339)

05

A DIFFERENT KIND OF SUMMARY

05 ⟩ A DIFFERENT KIND OF SUMMARY: SEEING THE BIGGER PICTURE

> *What drives us? The around-the-clock search for the ultimate (passing game) training and game, true professionalism with a strong leaning towards self-perfection, and the desire to bring along others on the path to the game of games.*
> (Hyballa and te Poel)

The entire soccer world is talking about Barcelona's wonderful *Tiqui-Taca*, FC Bayern Munich's attractive and very successful *flat and combination pass game* during the 2012/2013 season, the extremely successful continuation of Munich's collective but varied and successful soccer under Pep Guardiola during the 2013/2014 season (German national champions, DFB Cup champions, and world champions), and Borussia Dortmund's surprising killer pass game under the German soccer instructor Jürgen Klopp. One usually associates this with a passing game as a requirement for attractive and result-oriented soccer that delights many spectators around the world.

Even a "soccer god" like Pelé is already asking the protagonists of the current soccer Bundesliga and the national team in commercials to preserve the exclusive right (of Brazilian soccer) to a light-footed and technically sophisticated and delightful soccer game.

Respect and esteem must be earned. Everything has its price, even from a temporal, textual, and methodical point of view. It is therefore important, particularly in professional training, to continuously scrutinize basic and key performance factors. What is behind this magical passing game of present day outstanding teams and national teams with respect to content and methods, and how can that really be trained, practiced, and taught on the training ground? We have attempted to answer this question with many of their own playing variations and drills, but not all passes are created equal, and quality does not fall into someone's lap!

Based on this fundamental assumption and taking into account theoretical game considerations and situational game findings, we developed our own teaching approach known as the Hyballa/te Poel Passing Puzzle IQ®. It is intended as a custom review of the very diverse and often neglected passing game, to be used for training at all playing levels, and to be effectively used in its many different variants on the training ground.

Furthermore, in a second German book about the passing game that has been published in 2015, the authors will present for the training of coaches and instructors on the field

- numerous best practice examples with interviews on the passing game from an international perspective,
- an attractive and practice-oriented model of a school that teaches ball games to young children,
- an insight into the workings of a world-class technique shop,
- detailed practice forms for passing schools of top trainers and clubs, and
- the point of view of the well-known sport scientist (with special expertise in soccer) of Dr. D. Memmert (German Sports College Cologne).

The selection of topics will be presented to the interested public at large in an appropriate and non-ideological manner and without claiming completeness, by means of explanation, illustration, and interpretation of the our own teaching model, the Hyballa/te Poel Passing Puzzle IQ®. May each interested reader draw his or her own conclusions.

In the future, we are considering a more intensive practical implementation of our own teaching model and the continuation of the chosen methodical and textual approach to other key performance factors in soccer.

Furthermore we discuss issues that will be more closely examined in the future:

- What does the passing game of the future look like? Does it have even more speed; can neural networks be the answer to this question?
- Highly intensive interval training (HIT) and passing training? How can both areas be reconciled in terms of learning and training or rather structuring stress and strain during the training process?
- The pros and cons of 11-0 passing play?
- Long-term work in the sense of training to become a pro soccer player (via soccer instructors and coaches) with the Hyballa/te Poel Passing Puzzle IQ®. Who is interested in a long-term field test?
- The role of the coach and instructor in today's modern passing game? Observer, admonisher, guide, and with what effective methodical inventory?

In closing, we would like to cite quotations from three different sources on these complex topics that could not have been said any better:

> **kicker:** *What is important in soccer?*
>
> **Lucien Favre (Head coach Borussia Mönchengladbach):** *"The problem is obvious: Space is tight, and solutions must be found to be able to go deep. This requires patience and precision. And intelligence. Playing intelligence is important; the game must be read and anticipated. Otherwise it gets difficult. It takes the right*

balance between technique, athleticism, and running ability. And the mindset must be right.

kicker: *You always talk about precision.*

Lucien Favre (Head coach Borussia Mönchengladbach): *Yes, take the passing game for example. The quality of passes is important to me. How can I play quickly when the balls are sloppy? That doesn't work! The pass has to be accurate and played clean and at the right moment."*

(Lucien Favre in a kicker interview with H. Hasselbruch and J. Lustig, 2011, "Netzer is Right" 22, pg. 10-13)

"Only when one first gets completely wrapped up in the details like a wild man is one sometimes rewarded with moments of complete lightness. It is similar to a great violinist. Whenever he plays the violin so easily and everyone feels like they might be able to fly. He actually worked his fingers to the bone on that."

(Christian Streich, head coach of Bundesliga and European League team FC Freiburg, quoted in Memmert et al. 2013, pg. 215)

"Creation is never complete. It did start once. But it will never end."

(Immanuel Kant)

And that's the end of it.

Köln and Leverkusen, Germany, May 2014

06 ⌐ REFERENCES

"The trick is to work really hard every day, even during the week. Staying immune to those ever-present base flatteries."

(Fredi Bobic, Manager VfB Stuttgart and 37-time national team player, with 285 Bundesliga games, 108 scored goals, and part of the magic triangle)

Abel, G. (2004). Zeichen der Wirklichkeit. Frankfurt am Main: Suhrkamp.

Aebli, H. (1980). Denken: Das Ordnen des Tuns. Band I. Stuttgart: Klett-Cotta.

Aebli, H. (1981). Denken: Das Ordnen des Tuns. Band II. Stuttgart: Klett-Cotta.

Arroyo, R. O. (1992). Teoria del Fútbol. Wanceulen Deporitva Editorial S. L.

Arroyo, R. (2002): Fußballtheorie. http://www.soccertheory.com/german/primitiv. htm. Accessed on 10th July 2013.

Arts, M. (2013). Positionsspiel des Torhüters und Defensivverhalten bei Freistößen und Eckstößen – Zusammenspiel von Torhütern und Feldspielern. In: BUND DEUTSCHER FUSSBALL-LEHRER (Ed.). Internationaler Trainer-Kongress 2013. Individualisierung des Trainings: Eine Voraussetzung für Höchstleistung im Fußball. Frankfurt am Main, pp. 32-37.

Ausubel, D. (1974). Psychologie des Unterrichts. Band 1 und 2. Weinheim: Beltz.

Ball, K. (2008). Foot interaction during kicking in Australian Rules Football. In Science and football VI, (edited by Reilly, T. and Korkusuz, F.), pp. 36-40. London: Routledge.

Barfield, WR. (1998). The biomechanics of kicking in soccer. Clinic Sports Medicine. 17 (4), pp. 711-728.

Baumann, S. (2008). Mannschaftspsychologie. Methoden und Techniken. Aachen: Meyer & Meyer.

Bechthold, A. (2014). Coaching aus Trainersicht. Leistungssport, 2, pp. 22-26.

Bechthold, A. & Otto, M. (2014). "Wenn er mich anschreit, kann ich mich gar nicht mehr aufs Spiel konzentrieren!" fussballtraining, 1/2, pp. 22- 27.

Bernreuther, D. (2013). "So können wir nicht weitermachen". kicker, 61, p. 31.

Bisanz, G. & Gerisch, G. (2013). Fussball. Kondition, Technik, Taktik & Coaching. Aachen: Meyer & Meyer.

Bischof, R. (1985). Das Rätsel Ödipus. Die biologischen Wurzeln des Urkonflikts zwischen Begegnung und Autonomie. München, Zürich. Piper.

Buschmann, J., Kollath, E. & Tritschoks, H-J. (2005). Gezielt trainieren – erfolgreich spielen. Band 1. WEKA MEDIA GmbH & Co. KG.

Carling, C. & Dupont, G. (2011). Are declines in physical performance associated with a reduction in skill-related performance during professional soccer match-play? In. Journal of Sports Sciences, 299, pp. 63-71.

Daniel, J. (2013). Ruhig mal Querdenken. In. fussballtraining, 1 und 2, pp. 34-41.

Daniel, J. (2014). Spielen, Üben, Spielen. fussballtraining, 1/2, pp. 52-53.

Dante (02.12.2013). Quoted in kicker-Interview with Zitouni, M., p. 13

Dieterle, Cl. (10th February 2014). Der geliebte Pedant. Frankfurter Allgemeine Zeitung, 34, p. 12.

Dost, H., te Poel, H.-D. & Hyballa, P. (2015). Fußballfitness: Athletiktraining. Aachen: Meyer & Meyer Verlag.

Duden (1996). Wörterbuch der deutschen Rechtsschreibung. Mannheim; Leipzig; Wien; Zürich: Dudenverlag.

Eichler, Ch. (28th April 2014). Münchener Hilferuf. Braucht Bayern jetzt Deutschland? Frankfurter Allgemeine Zeitung, 98, p. 23.

Eichler, Ch. (o.J.). Frankfurter Allgemeine Sonntagszeitung, o.S..

Eichler, Ch. (4th February 2014). Eine Ode an die Bayern. Frankfurter Allgemeine Zeitung, 29, p. 23.

Elgert, N. (28th April 2014). Quoted in Interview with Müller, T. "Erfolg braucht ein Fundament" im kicker, 36, pp. 78-79.

Favre, L. (2011). Quoted in Interview mit von Hasselbruch & Lustig, J. in kicker, 22, pp. 10-13.

Favre, L. (22nd November 2013). Quoted in Interview with Marx, U. and Leipold, R. in the Frankfurter Allgemeinen Zeitung, 272, p. 29.

Ferrauti, A., Knoop, M., Pitschetsrieder, H. & Streibig, D.d.C. (2009). Entwicklung einer Testbatterie für den Fußball-Torhüter. Leistungssport, 4, pp. 16-22.

FIFA (2010). 2010 FIFA World Cup South Africa. Technical Report and Statistics. Zürich.

FIFA (2011). FIFA U17-World Cup Mexico 2011. Technical Report and Statistics. Zürich.

Frankfurter Allgemeinen Zeitung (22nd November 2013). 272, p. 29.

Frankfurter Allgemeine Zeitung (25th November 2013). 274, p. 13.

Frey, G. & Hildenbrandt, E. (1995). Grundlagen der Trainingslehre. Band 2: Anwendungsfelder. Schorndorf: Hofmann.

Furley, P. & Memmert, D. (2013). "Whom Should I Pass To?" The More Options the More Attentional Guidance from Working Memory. PloS One 8(5): e62278. http://dx.plos.org./10.1371/journal.pone.0062278. Accessed on 14th September 2013.

fussballtraining (Red.) (2013). Viele Wege führen ins Tor. 5, Münster: Philippka, pp. 6-7.

Guardiola, P. (3rd May 2014). Quoted in the Frankfurter Neuen Presse, 102, p. 8.

Guilford, J.P. (1967). The Nature of Human Intelligence. New York: McGraw-Hill.

Hartmann, O. (2nd February 2015). "Ab Sommer nur noch Leipzig". kicker, 12, pp. 20-21.

Hänsel, F., Werkmann, S., Schulz, C. & Kappes, E. (2013). Trainings- und Wettkampfqualität aus Athleten- und Trainersicht – Unterschiede und Gemeinsamkeiten. Leistungssport, 6, pp. 16-22.

Hänsel, F. & Baumgärtner, S. D. (2014). Training des Zusammenspiels in Sportspielen. In K. Zentgraf & J. Munzert (Eds.). Kognitives Training im Sport, pp. 37-62. Göttingen: Hogrefe.

Hegen, P. & Schöllhorn, W.I. (2012a). Gleichzeitig in verschiedenen Bereichen besser werden, ohne zu wiederholen? Paralleles differenzielles Training von zwei Techniken im Fußball. Leistungssport, 3, pp. 17-23.

Hegen, P. & Schöllhorn, W.I. (2012b). Lernen an Unterschieden und nicht durch Wiederholung. fussballtraining, 3, pp. 30-37.

Hehl, S. (2014). Saisonplanung: Orientieren Sie sich an den Stützpunkten! fussballtraining, 1/2, pp. 54-61.

Helms, M. (8th August 2013). Das Duell der „Dinos". Frankfurter Neue Presse, p. 9.

Heuer, A. (2012). Der perfekte Tipp. Weinheim: Wiley.

Hildebrand, T. (8th November 2013). Quoted in the Frankfurter Allgemeinen Zeitung, 260, p. 31.

Höhner, O. (23rd June 2005). Kopf ab zum Schuss. DIE ZEIT, p. 36.

Hoffmann, J. (1993). Vorhersage und Erkenntnis. Die Funktion von Antizipationen in der menschlichen Verhaltenssteuerung und Wahrnehmung. Göttingen: Hogrefe.

Hordijk, M. (2012). Technik, Technik und noch einmal Technik. fussballtraining, 12, pp. 6-15.

Hossner, E.-J. (2002). Bewegte Ereignisse – ein Versuch über die menschliche Motorik. Unveröffentlichte Habilitationsschrift, Universität Heidelberg.

Hossner, E.-J. (2005). Sportspiel aus bewegungswissenschaftlicher Sicht. In Hohmann, A., Kolb, M. & Roth, K. (Eds.). Handbuch Sportspiel. Schorndorf: Verlag Karl Hofmann, pp. 116-131.

Hyballa, P. & te Poel, H.-D. (2013). Mythos niederländischer Nachwuchsfußball. Aachen: Meyer & Meyer. 2nd edition.

Hyballa, P. & te Poel, H.-D. (2013b). Am 1-4-3-3-System orientieren! In fussballtraining, 12, pp. 40-46.

Juárez D, Mallo J, De Subijana C & Navarro E. (2011). Kinematic analysis of kicking in young top-class soccer players. Journal Sports Medicine Physical Fitness, 51 (3). pp. 366-73.

Kibele, A. (2013). Elfmeter – zum aktuellen Forschungsstand einer bedeutsamen Standardsituation im Fußballspiel. Leistungssport, 6, pp. 46-50.

Kluge, Fr. (1999). Etymologisches Wörterbuch der deutschen Sprache. Berlin; New York: de Gruyter.

Knievel, G. (2011). FIFA WM 2010: Kreativität und Torerziehung. Unpublished diploma thesis, DSHS Köln.

Kollath, E. (2000). Fußball, Technik & Taktik. Aachen: Meyer & Meyer.

Kuhl, J. (2001). Motivation und Persönlichkeit. Göttingen: Hogrefe.

Lahm, Ph. (7th November 2013). Quoted in the Frankfurter Allgemeinen Zeitung, 259, p. 24.

Lames, M. (2012). Videotaktiktraining - unausgeschöpfte Potenziale? In DFB (Ed.). Neue Trends bei der EURO 2012: Entscheidungskompetenz in Abwehr und Angriff. Frankfurt am Main, pp. 41-47.

Lames, M. (1999). Fußball – Ein Chaosspiel:. In Jansen, J.-P., Wegner, W. & M. (Eds.). Empirische Forschung im Sportspiel – Methodologie, Fakten und Reflektionen. Kiel: Christian-Alberts-Universität zu Kiel, pp. 141-156.

Leipold, R. (23.09.2013). Die Wege der Bayern sind unergründlich. Frankfurter Allgemeine Zeitung, p. 15.

Lieberknecht, T. (22.7.2013). Quoted in kicker according to Bernreuther, p. 31.

Linz, L. (2006). Erfolgreiches Teamcoaching. Aachen: Meyer & Meyer.

Löw, J. (March 2012). Quoted in 11FREUNDE, 124, p. 33.

Löw, J. (10th March 2014). "Manuel hat eine unglaubliche Ausstrahlung". kicker, 22, p. 6.

Loy, R. (2012). Zufall im Fußball, eine empirische Untersuchung zur Art und Auftretenshäufigkeit zufälliger Ereignisse im Verlauf von Fußballspielen. In Jansen, C.T., Baumgart, C., Hoppe, M.W. & Freiwald, J. (Eds.). Trainingswissenschaftliche, geschlechtsspezifische und medizinische Aspekte des Hochleistungsfußballs. Beiträge und Analysen zum Fußballsport XVIII. Hamburg: Cwalina, pp. 28-38.

Lutz, H. (2010). Besser Fußball spielen mit Life Kinetik. BLV: München.

Luhukay, J. (9th September 2013). "Meine Frau sagt: Jos, eigentlich bist du ein bekloppter Mensch". Interview with Röser, U. & J.-J. Beer im kicker, 74, pp. 12-15.

McClelland, J. L., Rumelhart, D. E., & The PDP Research Group. (1986). Parallel distributed processing (Vol. 2). Cambridge, MA: MIT Press.

Meijer, M. (2006). GUUS HIDDINK. Going Dutch. Random House Australia.

Memmert, D. (2003). Kognitionen im Sportspiel. Unpublished dissertation. Heidelberg.

Memmert, D. (2004). Kognitionen im Sportspiel. Köln: Sport & Buch Strauß.

Memmert, D. (2005). Komplextraining. In Hohmann, A., Kolb, M. & Roth, K. (Eds.). Handbuch Sportspiel. Schorndorf: Verlag Karl Hofmann, pp. 359-364.

Memmert, D. (2006). Optimales Taktiktraining im Leistungsfußball. Band 1. Balingen: Spitta Verlag GmbH & Co. KG.

Memmert, D. (2012a). Kreativität im Sportspiel. Sportwissenschaft, 42, pp. 38-49.

Memmert, D. (2012b). Kreativitätsförderung im Sport-Spiel-Unterricht. In König, St., Memmert. D. & Kolb, M. (Eds.) (2012). Sport-Spiel-Unterricht. Band 1. Berlin: Logos Verlag, pp. 21-32.

Memmert, D. (2013a). Laufen die Spieler in England mehr als in Spanien? kicker, 28, p. 95.

Memmert, D. (2013b). Unterscheidet sich England in der Pass-Statistik von Spanien. kicker, 66, p. 95.

Memmert, D. (2013c). Haben Profis einen „anderen" Blick auf das Geschehen? kicker, 70, p. 91.

Memmert, D. (2013d). Wo steckt die Kreativität – im Assist oder vorletzten Pass. kicker, 44, p. 103.

Memmert, D. & Roth, K. (2003). Individualtaktische Leistungsdiagnostik im Sportspiel. Spectrum der Sportwissenschaften, 15, pp. 44-70.

Memmert, D., Strauss, B. & Theweleit, D. (2013). DER FUSSBALL – DIE WAHRHEIT. München: Süddeutsche Zeitung Edition.

Memmert, D., Hüttermann, S., Hagemann, N., Loffing, F. & Strauss, B. (2013). Dueling in the Penalty Box: Evidence-Based Recommendations on How Shooters and Goalkeepers Can Win Penalty Shootouts in Soccer. International Review of Sport and Exercise Psychology, 6, pp. 209-229.

Merz, D. & Thiel, A. (2014). Kommunikation zwischen Trainer und Athlet. Studie zu Einzelgesprächen im Spitzensport. Leistungssport, 1, pp. 39-45.

Möhlmann; B. (8th August 2013). Quoted in kicker according to Helms, M., p. 9.

Mourinho, J. (20th January 2014). Quoted in kicker by Wild, K, & Zitouni, M., 8, p. 6.

Müller, Th. (10th October 2013). Quoted in Interview with Kamp, Ch. in the Frankfurter Allgemeinen Zeitung, p. 24.

Naito K., Fukui Y. & Maruyama T. (2010). Multijoint kinetic chain analysis of knee extension during the soccer instep kick. Human Movement Science. 29 (2), pp. 59-76.

Neue Nassauische Presse (1st February 2014). Der Charaktertest. Bert van Marwijk sucht die richtigen Spieler für den Abstiegskampf. 27, p. 7.

Neuer, M. (5th March 2014). "Zu null, das muss unsere WM-Grundlage sein". Interview with Horeni, M. in the Frankfurter Allgemeinen Zeitung, 54, p. 28.

Neuer, M. (7th April 2014). "Die große Show ist nicht mein Ding". kicker, 30, pp. 10-11.

Neumaier, A., te Poel, H.-D. & Standtke, V. (1987). Zur Antizipation des Elmetertorschusses aus der Sicht des Torwarts. Leistungssport, 5, pp. 23-32.

Neumaier, A. (1999). Koordinatives Anforderungsprofil und Koordinationstraining. Köln: Sport und Buch Strauß.

Neumaier, A. & Busch, C. (i.D.). Koordinationstraining des Fußballtorwarts. Köln: Sport und Buch Strauß.

Nitsch, J. R. (1997). Kollektive Entscheidungen im Sportspiel – eine Problemskizze. In Konzag, G. (Ed.). Psychologie im Sportspiel. Köln: bps-Verlag, pp. 41-62.

Nitsch, J. R. (2004). Die handlungstheoretische Perspektive: ein Rahmenkonzept für die sportpsychologische Forschung und Intervention. Sportpsychologie, 11 (1), pp. 10-23.

Novoisky, C., Beyer, C.-N., Zepperitz, S. & Büsch, D. (2012). Ein trainingsmethodisches und technologisches Konzept zum Video-Feedback im Techniktraining. Leistungssport, 6, pp. 19-25.

Oliver, N. (1996). Techniktraining unter konditioneller Belastung. Schorndorf: Hofmann.

Pellegrini, M. (02. Oktober 2013). Quoted in the Frankfurter Allgemeinen Zeitung, p. 28.

Popper, K.R. (1995). Alles Leben ist Problemlösen. Über die Erkenntnis, Geschichte und Politik. München, Zürich: Piper.

Potthast, W., Heinrich, K., Schneider, J. & Brueggemann, G.-P. (o.J.). The Success of a Soccer Kick Depends on Run up Deceleration. o.O.

Raab, M. (2000). SMART. Techniken des Taktiktrainings – Taktiken des Techniktrainings. Köln: Sport und Buch Strauß.

Raads, St. (2009). Theorie der Handlungsschnelligkeit im Sportspiel Fußball. Unpublished dissertation. Osnabrück.

Rechner, M. & Memmert, D. (2010). Das technisch-taktische Anforderungsprofil des modernen Fußballtorwarts – Die 5x3 Top-Basics des Torwartspiels. Leistungssport, 4, pp. 32 ff.

Robben, A. (1st November 2013). Quoted in the Frankfurter Allgemeinen Zeitung, 254, p. 30.

Roth, G. (2009). Aus Sicht des Gehirns. Berlin: Suhrkamp Verlag.

Roth, K. (1996). Techniktraining im Spitzensport. Köln: Sport und Buch Strauß.

Roth, K. (2005a). Sportspiel-Vermittlung. In Hohmann, A., Kolb, M. & Roth, K. (Eds.). Handbuch Sportspiel. Schorndorf: Verlag Karl Hofmann, pp. 290-308.

Roth, K. (2005b). Techniktraining. In Hohmann, A., Kolb, M. & Roth, K. (Eds.). Handbuch Sportspiel. Schorndorf: Verlag Karl Hofmann, pp. 335-341.

Roth, K. (2005c). Taktiktraining. In Hohmann, A., Kolb, M. & Roth, K. (Eds.). Handbuch Sportspiel. Schorndorf: Verlag Karl Hofmann, pp. 342-349.

Roxburgh, A. (2012). Erfolg im Fußball: die Trends im Spitzenbereich. In DFB (Ed.). Neue Trends bei der EURO 2012: Entscheidungskompetenz in Abwehr und Angriff. Frankfurt am Main, pp. 6-12.

Rutemöller, E. (2010). Das Spiel lesen lernen! Die Wahrnehmung in Raum und Zeit unter Zeit- und Gegnerdruck verbessern. fussballtraining, 9, p. 40 f.

Rybicki, M. (2013). Vom Feldwebel-Sepp zum Freidenker-Pep. In Nassausische Neue Presse, 190, p. KuS 1.

Schöllhorn, W.I., Sechelmann, M., Trockel, M, & Westers, R. (2006). Nie das Richtige trainieren, um richtig zu spielen. Leistungssport, 5, pp. 13-17.

Schöllhorn, W.I., Beckmann, H. & Michelbrink, M. (2013). System(at)ische Betrachtungen von Trainingsprinzipien. Leistungssport, 3, pp. 5-10.

Schulze-Marmeling, D. (2013). Guardiola. Der Fußball-Philosoph. Göttingen: Die Werkstatt.

Schwab, S. (2013). Motivation und Stress. – Die Analyse von Stress mit einem speichelbasierten Biomarker in einer motivationalen Fit-Situation unter Berücksichtigung von Leistungsparametern. Köln: Unpublished dissertation, DSHS.

Schweinsteiger, B. (14th October 2013). Quoted in kicker-Interview by Hartmann, O. & Wild, K., p. 10.

Seeger, F. (2008). Coaching im Wettkampfsport. Eine empirische Untersuchung im Fußball. Hamburg: Diplomica® Verlag GmbH.

Siegle, M., Geisel, M. & Lames, M. (2012). Zur Aussagekraft von Positions- und Geschwindigkeitsdaten im Fußball. Deutsche Zeitschrift für Sportmedizin, 63, pp. 278-282.

Sorg, M. (17th September 2013). Quoted in the Frankfurter Allgemeinen Zeitung, p. 29.

Spitzer, M. (2006). Lernen: Gehirnforschung und die Schule des Lebens. Hamburg, Springer Verlag.

Streich, Ch. (27th August 2013). Quoted in the Frankfurter Neuen Presse, p. 7.

Süddeutsche.de (2013). Bundesliga Statistik. Gespielte Pässe in der Bundesliga-Saison 2012/2013. http://www.sueddeutsche.de/sport/bundesliga-statistik-gespielte-paesse-gespielte-paesse-in-der-bundesliga-saison--1.1592197. Accessed on 22nd July 2013.

Szymanski, B. (1997). Techniktraining in den Sportspielen – bewegungszentriert oder situationsbezogen? Hamburg: Czwalina.

Thaler. E. & Krebs, St. (2009). Der moderne Torhüter spielt mit! fussballtraining, 9, pp. 20-29.

te Poel, H.-D. (1984). Visuelle Wahrnehmung und Antizipation. Empirische Untersuchung zum Blick- und Entscheidungsverhalten beim Beobachten von Elfmetertorschüssen in Abhängigkeit von der Darbietungsgeschwindigkeit und der Beobachtungsanweisung. (Unpublished thesis), Institut für Bewegungs- und Trainingslehre, Deutsche Sporthochschule Köln.

te Poel, H.-D. & Hyballa, P. (2011). Wenn das Fußballtalent im Mathematikunterricht an den Doppelpass denkt! Wechselwirkungen zwischen Schule und Fußball im Leben eines zukünftigen Nationalspielers. Leistungssport, 4, pp. 33-38.

te Poel, H.-D. & Hyballa, P. (2015). Modernes Passspiel international. Aachen: Meyer & Meyer-Verlag.

Thiel, D. (2012). Drei Bausteine für den perfekten Keeper. In fussballtraining, 11, pp. 6-19.

Thaler, E. & Krebs, St. (2009). Der moderne Torhüter spielt mit. fussballtraining, 9, pp. 20-29.

Titz, C. & Dooley, Th. (2010). FUSSBALL. Passen und Ballkontrolle. Aachen: Meyer & Meyer.

UEFA (2012a). 2011/2012. Technischer Bericht UEFA Champions League. Nyon.

UEFA (2012b). 2012. Technischer Bericht UEFA EURO 2012 Poland-Ukraine. Nyon.

van Marwijk, B. (11th November 2013). Quoted in the Frankfurter Allgemeinen Zeitung, p. 13.

van Marwijk, B. (18th November 2013). Quoted in kicker-Interview with Wolff, p., 94, p. 43.

van Gaal, L. (2010). Vision. Dresden: Visiesport GmbH.

Voigt, L., Hohmann, A. & Singh, A. (2013). Konzepte erfolgreichen Nachwuchstrainings (KerN). Zentrale subjektive Trainertheorien zum leistungssportlichen Ausbildungsprozess. Leistungssport, 6, pp. 4-15.

von Nocks, St. (3rd February 2014). Wer mehr läuft, der gewinnt! Wer öfter den Ball hat, der gewinnt? Stimmt das eigentlich? kicker, 12, pp. 16-17.

Wahl, D. (1991). Handeln unter Druck: Weinheim: Deutscher Studien Verlag.

Wahl, D. (2006). Lernumgebungen erfolgreich gestalten. Bad Heilbrunn: Klinkhardt.

Wahl, D. (2012). Ergebnisse der lernpsychologischen Forschung: Konsequenzen für die Gestaltung des Sport-Spiel-Unterrichts. In: König, St., Memmert, D. & Kolb, M. (Eds.). Sport-Spiel-Unterricht. Berlin: Logos Verlag, pp. 53-73.

Wawrinka, S. (11th November 2013). Quoted in the Frankfurter Allgemeinen Zeitung, p. 15.

Wein, H. (2004). Developing game intelligence in soccer. Spring City: Reedswain.

Weineck, J., Memmert, D. & Uhing, M. (2012). Optimales Koordinationstraining im Fußball. Balingen: Spitta Verlag GmbH & Co. KG.

Wild, Kh. (7th October 2013). kicker, p. 19.

Winner, D. (2008). Oranje brilliant. Das neurotische Genie des holländischen Fußballs. Köln: Kiepenheuer und Wietsch.

Wolfrum, J. (2013). Der Denker. kicker, 62, pp. 68-69.

Wollny, R. (2002). Motorische Entwicklung in der Lebensspanne. Schorndorf: Hofmann.

Wormuth, F. (2011). Das große Spiel entscheidet sich im Detail. In: Bund Deutscher Fußball-Lehrer (Ed.). Internationaler Trainer-Kongress 2011, pp. 43- 47.

Wormuth, F. (2013). Wann trainiere ich das taktische Verhalten? fussballtraining, 3, pp. 6-13.

Wulf, G. & Prinz, W. (2001). Directing attention to movement effects enhances learning. A review. Psychological Bulletin & Review, 8, pp. 648-660.

Zitouni, M. & Wild, Kh. (7th April 2014). Riskantes Spiel. kicker, 30, pp. 44-45.

CREDITS

Graphics:

Eduard Feldbusch (German Sports College Cologne, with a degree in training and performance) /www.sports-graphics.com

Photos:

©picture-alliance/dpa: Pg. 71, 98, 105, 106, 111, 128, 145, 153, 197, 210, 232, 239, 252, 275, 347, 380, 390

Hyballa/te Poel: all other photos

Jacket graphic: ©thinkstock/photos.com

Copyediting:	Elizabeth Evans
Layout:	Cornelia Knorr
Typesetting & Jacket:	Eva Feldmann
Cover:	Andreas Reuel
Jacket:	Sannah Inderelst

FURTHER BOOKS ABOUT SOCCER

Timo Jankowski

SUCCESSFUL GERMAN SOCCER TACTICS

The Best Match Plans for a Winning Team

A match plan describes a strategy that is used to be ideally prepared for the next match and be able to react to shifts in tactics or to particular match situations.

This book aims to provide every soccer aficionado with a practical insight into the topics of match ideas, tactics, match systems, and match plans using easy-to-understand language.

248 p., in color, 58 photos,

50 illus., paperback,

6 1/2" x 9 1/4"

ISBN: 9781782550624

$ 16.95 US/$ 29.95 AUS/

£ 12.95 UK/€ 16.95

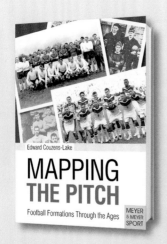

Edward Couzens-Lake

MAPPING THE PITCH

Football Formations Through the Ages

This book is an entertaining exploration of the history and evolution of football formations from the Victorian age gentleman 'players' to the successes—and failures—of the 2014 World Cup in Brazil. The author analyses the thinking behind the popular formations and shows how the thinking behind the game changed in football from the late 19th century onwards.

c. 300 p., b/w, c. 40 photos
+ illus., paperback,
5 3/4" x 8 1/4"

ISBN: 9781782550600

c. $ 14.95 US/$ 22.95 AUS/
£ 9.95 UK/€ 14.95

MEYER & MEYER
Fachverlag
Von-Coels-Str. 390
52080 Aachen
Germany

Phone	+49 02 41 - 9 58 10 - 13
Fax	+49 02 41 - 9 58 10 - 10
E-Mail	sales@m-m-sports.com
Website	www.m-m-sports.com

All books available as E-books.

MEYER
& MEYER
SPORT